A. E. H.

My Brother, A. E. HOUSMAN: Personal Recollections Together with Thirty Hitherto Unpublished Poems

By

LAURENCE HOUSMAN

With Eight Full-page Illustrations

NEW YORK
CHARLES SCRIBNER'S SONS
1938

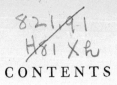

CONTENTS

ILLUSTRATIONS

INTRODUCTION

THESE personal recollections of my brother, A. E. Housman, and the few literary remains which go with them, have no claim to be regarded as a biography. I do not think that a complete life of him could ever be written, except in a collaboration which I might name, but which is hardly likely to materialize. His life of seventy-seven years divided itself rather definitely into sections; and those among his survivors who knew him either intimately or through daily intercourse, knew him only in one, or at most in one-and-a-half of those separated periods. I myself knew very little of his life in its day-to-day activities after he left home for Oxford, where he made his greatest and most lasting friendship with one who died in 1923, and left no record of their association. Others knew him, but not intimately, during the ten years which he spent as a Civil Servant at the Patent Office; others knew him in more congenial surroundings during the following nineteen years of his professorship at University College, London; and others, a much larger number, during the remaining twenty-five years of his life when, as a resident Fellow of Trinity College, Cambridge, he filled the post of Kennedy Professor of Latin.

Of this last period the one best qualified to give a

record, both by intimate knowledge and warm friend-ship, Mr. A. S. F. Gow, one of his co-Fellows at Trinity, has published an admirable study (*A. E. Housman: A Sketch*. The University Press, Cambridge) on which, as it covers the ground so well, I shall try not to encroach. There is also the memorial number of *The Broms-grovian* (published by The Bookshop, Bromsgrove School) which contains contributions by friends and relations dealing with different aspects and periods of his life, especially that of his boyhood written by his sister, Mrs. Katharine E. Symons.

Probably the person (other than members of his own family) whose intercourse with my brother extended over the widest range of years was his friend and publisher Mr. Grant Richards, who also has published a record of their association, mainly in hours of leisure, spent in travel and conviviality.

But though the two friends I have named are well qualified to write of those parts of my brother's life with which they were in contact, a full biography lies outside the range of any single writer known to me; and where the attempt at such a production has been made, it has been without due qualification and with results which I deprecate.

Three years before his death, my brother wrote to a correspondent: 'If I write anything of an autobiographical nature, as I have sometimes idly thought of doing, I shall send it to the British Museum to be kept under lock and key for fifty years.' To this he added: 'There is no biography of Matthew Arnold, so there certainly need be none of me.'

Even before making inquiry, I was sufficiently sure that the 'idle thought' had never materialized. Official assurance from the British Museum has confirmed my confidence that nothing of an autobiographical nature lies there in cold storage for the delectation of a future generation.

This statement will, I hope, put an end to one of the items of journalistic nonsense which have found circulation since my brother's death. There is a certain type of mind which always tries to turn reticence into mystery. A.E.H. was a shy, proud, and reticent character; even to his intimates he was provokingly reserved, finding, I think, a certain pleasure in baffling injudicious curiosity. Out of that reserve the journalistic mind has endeavoured to construct a hidden romance which was non-existent, and to suggest that some 'lost lady of old years' was the cause of the secluded and celibate life which he adopted in early manhood, and persisted in till the end. Against that I can only state my conviction that A.E.H. was a born bachelor; and that he chose the habit of life which best suited him.

He was not a man of happy disposition; but in spite of that handicap, he extracted from life a good deal of melancholy satisfaction suited to his temperament; and though he smiled at life somewhat wryly, he did manage to smile; and it was noticeable to his friends that even though his mirth was somewhat ironical, he had the gift of happy and musical laughter. One of these friends has described it as 'bell-like': that is quite true: it rang a musical peal and was, like the bells on Bredon, 'a happy noise to hear'. When he was thoroughly amused – as he often was – it went on and on; and when in his last years he paid visits to his invalid brother, Dr. Basil Housman, the report was that, even from downstairs, they could be heard laughing together, and the laughter was loud and long. It was to this brother that he sent, for his amusement, year by year, the nonsense verses, some of which are here printed for the first time; and it was that same brother who in early years, taking French leave, published in our school magazine, *The Bromsgrovian*, the one and only story which Alfred ever wrote, but which, under his instructions about his prose writings, I am unable to republish.

With regard to the other material – letters, verses, and bibliographical notes – which accompany this memoir, a few words of explanation are due. Of my brother's letters I have made no attempt to make a collection; those which I give here, addressed mainly to near relatives, I have included as a commentary upon our personal and family relations; and also as illustrating – better perhaps than a more miscellaneous collection would do – the curious precision and abruptness of his style as a correspondent, even when writing to his familiars.

The verses here collected fall under two headings. It is quite obvious that those which may be classed as nonsense verses would have been out of place in *More Poems*; but as he had already given permission during his lifetime, to myself and others, to republish several of them, I have felt justified in now making a larger selection, while still keeping to a certain standard of limitation.

Of the other poems – the serious ones – which for various reasons I decided not to include in *More Poems*, more will be said later. My responsibility both of inclusion and exclusion in the editing of those left-over poems was very great, and in more instances than one I could find no satisfactory solution. Had I added a larger number, either of short pieces, single stanzas, or verses of a minor quality, their inclusion might have done harm to the selection as a whole. But, though it includes one poem which I would now rather have omitted, *More Poems* has in the estimation of most of its critics done its author's reputation no disservice; and in consequence I now feel myself more free to give separately in this memoir a few remaining pieces, about the publication of which I was in the first instance doubtful.

I have also made a detailed analysis of the contents of the four note-books which I am under orders to destroy, in which the bulk of my brother's poems were written – my desire being to preserve, as far as is permissible, material which will be of service to students, bearing mainly upon the dates and sequence of composition of all the now-published poems.

I have to thank Sir Sydney Cockerell for the additional list of dates given him by my brother, many of which were not set down in the note-books; Mr. A. S. F. Gow for his friendly advice and assistance on many points where I might otherwise have gone astray; Mr. Percy Withers and the editor of *The New Statesman* for permission to quote from an article which appeared in its pages; the recipients of the letters here published for enabling me to make use of them; and Professor Broad for permission to reproduce the Natal Horoscope which he worked out for my brother a few years before his death.

L.H.

A MEMOIR

A MEMOIR

PARENTAGE, HOME LIFE, AND SCHOOL

ALFRED HOUSMAN was born on March 26th, 1859. He did not arrive without difficulty. Conditions arose which baffled the local doctor, and expert aid had to be called in. His mother, informed of her dangerous condition, made her own choice – not, as was suggested, a leading physician from Birmingham, but the country doctor from her old home at Woodchester, who had known her all her life, and – as she said – understood her. He was summoned by telegram, and on arrival secured a safe delivery after a further delay of twenty-four hours.

The house where this took place was not Perry Hall, Bromsgrove, which, a year later, became the family home, but a smaller one of Georgian date, the Valley House, Fockbury, two miles from the town. Facing it across the road was a fine cedar tree (now down), the branches of which almost touched the windows. When later the family returned for five years to Fockbury House, the home of our grandparents, the smaller house had become a girls' school, kept by three sisters whom we nicknamed Battle, Murder, and Sudden Death – suitable nomenclature for after-occupants of the house where the 'Shropshire Lad' had been born.

It was Alfred's boast that he could remember his own baptism – though only indirectly. His proof was that, at the age of two, he attended the baptism of his brother Robert: 'That', he declared, 'I can remember as if it were yesterday.' During the ceremony the thought struck him: 'But this is something I've seen before; only then they were doing it to me.' In recollecting that thought, he claimed recollection of the event itself, which actually took place on April 24th, 1859, before he was a month old. The probable explanation of his claim to have accomplished so incredible a feat of memory is that he confused Robert's christening with his own, when remembering his sister Clemence's, which came a year later.

That he had an extraordinarily accurate mind and a retentive memory there can be no doubt; but in his later years there were occasions when memory played him false; an instance of which occurs in the brief auto-biographical notes, which he gave to a French translator of some of his poems, with the following account of his birth, parentage, and upbringing:

'I was born in Worcestershire, not Shropshire, where I have never spent much time. My father's family was Lancashire and my mother's Cornish.' For this statement, as regards his mother, no justification can be found. All the family records go to show that her parents united true Devon blood with a Cotswold strain. Of his father's family Lancashire was the place of origin, but his grandmother Housman was born at Bromsgrove, Worces-

THE VALLEY HOUSE, FOCKBURY
WHERE A. E. H. WAS BORN

tershire, and his father at Kinver in the adjoining county of Stafford.

'I had', he goes on, 'a sentimental feeling for Shropshire because its hills were our western horizon. I know Ludlow and Wenlock, but my topographical details – Hughley, Abdon under Clee – are sometimes quite wrong. Remember that Tyrtaeus was not a Spartan. I took an interest in astronomy almost as early as I can remember; the cause, I think, was a little book we had in the house. I was brought up in the Church of England and in the High Church party, which is much the best religion I have ever come across. But Lemprière's Classical Dictionary, which fell into my hands when I was eight, attached my affections to paganism. I became a deist at 13 and an atheist at 21. I never had any scientific education. I wrote verse at eight or earlier, but very little until I was 35.'

That last statement needs qualification. He had a great facility for verse-writing, and not only wrote poems of a serious character, but was prolific in the kind of verse which is called 'nonsense'. In early years his compositions so much exceeded his own use for them, that he sometimes palmed them off on others; and my first sonnet, written when I was about six and before I knew what constituted a sonnet, was dragged out of me, or squeezed into me, by a process of hypnotic suggestion which left me entirely convinced at the time that the poem was mine, though I know better now. As other family sonnets were being written about the same time, I suspect that a similar thought-transference had been imposed more than once, in order that he might get rid of waste-products for which he had a tenderness, but did not wish to own.

Under his leadership, in a family of seven, we all wrote poems, even the unpoetic ones: lyrics, ballads, sonnets, narrative poems, nonsense rhymes, and compositions to which each contributed a verse (not always in the same metre) occupied a large part of our playtime alongside of the more active games of childhood, in which also, as often as not, he led and we followed.

I could not say whether his home life was as important to him as, under his inspiration, it was to us for the formation of interests which were to last through life; but as, in after years, he made the admiring comment, 'Was there ever such an interesting family as we were?', one may presume that, for him also, interest gave to those early associations a value that lasted.

To his early interest in astronomy I owe one of my own childish memories – an instance of how he found amusement in instructing others. One day he took two of us out on to the lawn, and there placed us as astronomical characters. I was the sun, my brother Basil the earth, Alfred was the moon. My part in the game was to stay where I was and rotate on my own axis; Basil's was to go round me in a wide circle rotating as he went; Alfred, performing the movements of the moon, skipped round him without rotation. And that is how I learned, and have ever since remembered, the primary relations of the sun, the earth, and the moon. I have a vague idea that he placed other members of the family at a farther remove to represent the more distant planets, but of this I am not sure. In the later years of our youth it was Robert, not Alfred, who gave most time to a study of the heavens, and devised for his own use a large telescope ingeniously made out of camera-lenses, which he filched from our father.

Alfred's early education was first under a governess (whom I can only remember by the caricatures which Alfred drew of her), then for about a year at a small dame-school, where a slipper was the regular instrument used for corporal punishment; this he, or another, one day threw up on to the school-roof in the vain hope that thereby corporal punishment would become abolished.

At the age of eleven, he was elected to a Foundation Scholarship at Bromsgrove School, where he remained to the end of his school-days. My memory of him there only begins when he had reached the sixth form, and, in his last term as head of the school, carried away most of his form's prizes.

During his early school-days he was still small for his age and also, probably, unusually quiet. This got him the nickname of Mouse, and bigger boys used to tread on him, pretending that they could not see him. Otherwise, he said, when speaking of his first school years, he had nothing much to complain of.

Alfred was away from home, spending his Easter holiday at Woodchester with old friends of our mother's, when, on his twelfth birthday, she died after a long and

painful illness. Her death had a profound effect upon him
for there had been between them a deep bond of affection
and understanding. As she neared her end she became
anxious lest his loss of her should affect his attitude to
religion; and when his father wrote to him telling him
of her death, there was something in the nature of a
message to that effect. It is more than likely – though
one can only guess – that what they feared did actually
happen; and that his early estrangement from the
religion of his childhood was caused by her death.

In all his after-life he spoke of her but seldom; but
three years ago when he and I were on holiday together,
he became more communicative than I had ever known
him before, both in regard to her and to other family
matters of interest only to ourselves. In that connection
he said a thing which struck me as indicating how early
in life his mind must have formed itself. We were
speaking of our mother, and, in answer to my question
whether he remembered her well: 'Oh, yes,' he said,
'she used to talk to me as if I were a grown-up person,
and told me many things of her early life.' During her
long illness, he also wrote her letters for her, some of
which are still in existence.

At the home of his Woodchester friends, the Wises,
with whom – so long as they lived – he remained in
constant intimacy, he met his most life-long friend, a
German lady named Sophie Becker. She was his senior
by about fifteen years; and was governess-companion
to the two daughters. When in late middle age she

A. E. HOUSMAN
AGED 5

A. E. HOUSMAN
AGED 2

returned to Germany, he continued to correspond with her; and when, a few years before his death, she died at the age of ninety, he expressed satisfaction at knowing that the last of his most intimate friends was safely out of a troublesome world.

This, I think, was one of his most comfortable friendships: I remember her coming to stay with us in 1874 – a dark and rather plain woman, but sharp, shrewd, sensible, and brightly humorous, just the right corrective (so far as it could be corrected) for the melancholic tendency which grew on him during his adolescent years.

Two years after our mother's death we moved to Fock-bury House, which had been the home of our Housman grandparents, and a few months later our father married again – a relative whom we had hitherto known as Cousin Lucy. She told me years afterwards that when she first consented to take on the management of, not seven, but six rather unruly children, Alfred, who had then passed from the unruly stage, wrote to assure her that he would do everything he could to help her in her difficult task. And he kept his word 'most loyally', she said. Nor can there be any doubt that his friendly mediation between the two generations, elder and younger, eased a situation which was sometimes difficult.

It was to our stepmother that he wrote one of the earliest of his letters which have been kept, when he paid his first visit to London during the Christmas holidays,

1874-5, giving a somewhat guide-book description of the things he was seeing. Of Epiphany Sunday he wrote: 'We went to the Chapel Royal for service – the Queen's present was given by an attenuated person with gorgeous trimmings who, Cousin Mary thinks, is an Earl, as there was one of those coronets on his carriage. Then we went to Trafalgar Square which is quite magical, and to Westminster. I explored the North transept where the statesmen are . . . and went into Poets' Corner. Service was at three with an anthem by Greene which was like a boa-constrictor – very long and very ugly.

'Yesterday I went to the British Museum and spent most of my time among the Greeks and Romans . . . What delighted me most was the Farnese Mercury. I examined some of the Nineveh bulls and lions, and I went through the Zoological Gallery . . . I have come to the conclusion, which you may tell to the readers of "the Centre of the Earth", that if the Mastodon and Megatherium were to fight, it would decidedly be a very bad job for the Megatherium. I may also remark that the Icthyosauri and Plesiosauri are by no means so large or terrific as those met by Professor Hardwigg and Co.

'I like the view from Westminster Bridge and Trafalgar Square best of all the *places* I have seen, and I am afraid you will be horrified to hear that I like St. Paul's better than Westminster Abbey. The Quadrant, Regent Street, and Pall Mall are the finest streets; but I think of all I have seen, what has impressed me most is – the Guards. This may be barbarian, but it is true.'

His high opinion of St. Paul's is puzzling, and was probably only temporary; for in later life he regarded Westminster Abbey as superior to Notre Dame, and never said much in praise of Renaissance architecture.

A fortnight later, just as he was returning to school, three members of the household were stricken with scarlet fever: and to avoid infection he became a temporary boarder. While thus cut off from the family he wrote to our stepmother giving a final account of his days in London, and then added: 'Yesterday I went into the Churchyard, from which one can see Fockbury quite plainly, especially the window of your room. I was there from 2 o'clock till 3. I wonder if you went into your room between those hours. One can see quite plainly the pine tree, the sycamore, and the elm at the top of the field. The house looks much nearer than you would expect, and the distance between the sycamore and the beeches in the orchard seems very great, much longer than one thinks it is when one is at Fockbury.'

Here, twenty years before the poems were written, is an incident which has in it the authentic note of the 'Shropshire Lad'. Even as a boy, separation from home surroundings affected him so much that it pleased him to spend from two to three of a winter's afternoon in viewing them from a distance. 'I wonder if you went into your room between those hours' is significant of the warm affection he already had for our stepmother, and always retained. It must have been only a few days afterwards, while the separation still lasted, that his shout came to us from across the adjacent meadow; on a half-holiday he had walked over to have news of us, and from the far hedge he shouted inquiries, to which we replied. I remember our stepmother walking across the field, depositing a potted plant for his inspection, then retiring to a safe distance while he looked at it, so that no possible infection could get to him.

So much has been made of the studied reticence and aloofness of his later years, that it is well to put on record that other side of his nature which always existed, however much he chose to conceal it.

Even before I came on the autobiographical note after his death, from which I have already quoted, I had guessed that Alfred's religion had never been much more than a formality. But once, in quite early days – on the principle, I suppose, of proving all things and holding only to that which was good -- he had given the Sermon on the Mount a practical trial. During some childish altercation his brother Robert smote him upon the cheek; he turned the other. Smitten upon that also, he threw the Sermon to the winds, and emerged from the subsequent conflict more victor than Christian. But he was not punitive in his treatment of his younger brothers, and I cannot remember his striking any of us except once. On our way to church one Sunday morning, he fell upon Robert and pummelled him for a persistent piece of teasing. My impression is that his fighting form was peculiarly unconvincing – mild, not furious; but Robert was so paralysed by astonishment that he put up

A. E. HOUSMAN (AGED 7)
AND HIS BROTHER ROBERT (AGED 5½)

no defence, fell into the hedge, and burst into tears. It was probably affectionate reverence as much as anything which overthrew the resistance of one who had himself a rather fiery temper; but it would have been almost like fighting a parent or an uncle to have stood against Alfred at that time as man to man.

A characteristic feature of Alfred's training of us was that, in our acquisition of taste and knowledge, he made us competitive and possessive. When he taught us the names of trees we each had to choose a favourite, but were not allowed to choose the same; and as a consequence we younger ones were fudged off with trees which we did not prefer. Alfred, I believe, chose the beech, and left the English oak for another.

Many years later he told me he was glad he had not been brought up in beech-wood country, for, had he been, its beauty would have made him unappreciative of any other kind.

Just as he roused our interest by dividing among us the trees of the forest, so did he lead us to share another of his early tastes, which lasted through life — his love of architecture. He had a photographic card, giving in miniature all the English cathedrals; and I remember how, even then, he knew a good deal about them, and was able to tell us, as he set us to choose our favourites, what were their main features and the reasons why we should desire them. St. Paul's was ruled out of the running; it was only Gothic that was to concern us; and as there were twenty-two in this style, we were each able

to have a first, second, and third choice. I am not sure
what his were, though I remember mine; but I know
that he did not then choose Wells which afterwards
became his favourite. As I write I have beside me the
card of photographs which gave him and us our first
interest in English cathedrals.

At the age of fourteen Alfred wrote the first of his
three school prize-poems, its subject – Sir Walter Raleigh.
This was followed in subsequent years by two other
poems, *The Death of Socrates*, and *Paul on Mars Hill*.
A few years ago he told me that he thought the first was
the best. It certainly was not. A declaration that the sun
tries in vain to catch up with the British Empire, which
'extends its rule sublime' all round the world, 'spanning
the seas', 'spurning the hurricanes', and bidding defiance
to all other nations, while tolling the knell of Spanish
tyranny 'when all creation formed its stool', is the prelude
to an exercise in youthful rhetoric, of which the only
worth-while lines are those describing the character of
James I:

> A King who sought the land to bind
> Down to the meanness of his mind,
> A man to coming times exempt
> From every feeling but contempt.

Apparently Alfred had not at that time acquired the
dislike for democracy and the acceptance of slavery as
necessary for civilization which in his later years inclined

him toward some form of benevolent despotism compatible with the liberty of thought which he valued above all things.

His two later poems were in much better style, more restrained in their rhetoric, well phrased though quite conventional, written in good, smooth heroic couplets – the regulation metre for prize-poems. Published by the local press in their prize-winning years, they are on record for the curious to discover, but not for re-publication as a whole; the best passage in *The Death of Socrates* is in the concluding lines:

Though weeping followers on the earth stand dumb
With sorrow, unto them no dawn has come,
On them no lifted veil has shed the light;
With lisping thought and visionary sight
They wait in twilight. But the day shall be
When a frail bark shall bear across the sea
One, in the wisdom of whose solemn eyes
A deeper, clearer well of light shall rise,
And on the hill thy feet so oft have trod,
He shall in fullness preach thine UNKNOWN GOD.

These represent his style at that date, when writing to order in a metre not of his own choosing.

Far more characteristic of what was to follow in later years are these verses written for a family competition, with 'The Oak' as their subject:

An acorn tumbled from the oak,
Who knows how many years ago,
How many years of nights and days?[1]
Perhaps when over woodland ways
The hoary Druid came and broke
The consecrated mistletoe.

And now the oak-tree throws a shadow
And bears an acorn of its own,
That ripens in its fairy cup,
Looking at heaven; and being grown
Falls rustling to the autumn meadow;
And pigs arise and eat it up.

This was followed by another competition – a poem on
the ruins of Rome:

The city is silent and solemn
    That once was alive and divine;
And here stands the shaft of a column,
    And there lies the wreck of a shrine;
But the wild bird still sings in the marshes,
    The wild flower still blooms on the lea,
And under its infinite arches
    The river runs down to the sea.

[1] This line is conjectural.

But the tide of the Tiber remembers
  A time which is long over-worn –
Saw Rome sinking down into embers,
  And flowed by her when she was born:
When the people were gathered for slaughter
  With Lucumo's princes and Lars,
And the bridge fell splashing the water
  High up to the turrets of Mars.

These were written when he was about sixteen; the following lines belong to about the same period or perhaps a little later:

Summer! and over brooding lands
A noonday haze of heat expands.
The gentle breeze along the meadows
Lifts a few leaflets on the trees,
But cannot stir the clouds that lie
Motionless on the dreaming sky,
And cannot shift the sleeping shadows
As motionless upon the leas.

Summer: and after summer, what?
Ah, happy trees, that know it not.
Would that with us it might be so!
And yet the broad-flung beech-tree heaves
Through all its slanting layers of leaves
With something of a sigh. Ah, no!
'Tis but the wind that with its breath
To them so softly murmureth:

For them hath still new sweets in store,
And sings new music evermore.
Only to us its tones seem sighs,
Only to us it prophesies
Of coming Autumn, coming death.

Here clearly, though conventional in treatment, is something not un-akin to what took form in *A Shropshire Lad* twenty years later. But it is a wonder and something of a mystery that a writer so prolific of verse in his teens should have produced so little during his twenties. Except for three poems written during his Oxford years (two of them published – the third, his attempt for the Newdigate Prize in 1879, not published) I have not been able to discover, even in the four note-books into which he jotted down the beginnings and rough drafts of his poems, any trace of a poem of earlier date than 1890.

Apropos of this long break in production, Sir Sydney Cockerell says that, in answer to a question whether when writing the poems of *A Shropshire Lad* he had at once realized their merit, he replied that he had, because they were so unlike anything that he had done previously.

This is noticeably true of 'New Year's Eve', the longer of the two poems which he published when at Oxford. It was written under the influence of Swinburne, but with a greater conciseness of phrase than was usually found in the imitators of that master of voluminous verse. These two stanzas give a sufficient indication of its style:

There stood in the holy places
A multitude none could name,
Ranks of dreadful faces
Flaming, transfigured in flame.

Crown and tiar and mitre
Were starry with gold and gem;
Christmas never was whiter
Than fear on the face of them.

It was a poem which, so far as it had any definite
meaning, indicated his conviction that Christianity was a
dying religion in which he himself had ceased to believe.

During Alfred's first three years at Bromsgrove
School, Dr. Blore, afterwards Head of King's School,
Canterbury, was his Headmaster; but though he had only
reached the fourth form when Dr. Blore left, his old
Head was said to have remembered him as the sort of
boy he was always afraid would ask him some question
he could not answer. Alfred himself doubted whether
this could be true, since Dr. Blore did not take the fourth
form in classics – the only subject, my brother thought,
in which he might have been able to ask stumping
questions. With Herbert Millington, Dr. Blore's successor, he got on exceedingly well. 'May all my boys
be like him!' was the valedictory sentence which
accompanied his last school report, when, as head of the
sixth form and having gained more prizes than any of
his contemporaries, he left school for Oxford.

35

My own relations with the Head having been less fortunate than his, I once asked him what he thought of Millington as a master. 'For clever boys with a taste for the classics', he said, 'excellent. For boys with less interest and of lower ability, quite the reverse.' As Alfred fulfilled the conditions which produced virtue, he had reason for an appreciation which others were not able to share.

Herbert Millington's appointment came shortly after our move to Fockbury, a move which, for Alfred – and later on for three others – entailed an early breakfast (six o'clock during summer term) and a walk in all weathers of over two miles morning and evening. But though this was somewhat of a hindrance to evening preparation, we thoroughly enjoyed our more rural surroundings; and it was there that Alfred began to take us walks and tell us the names of trees and flowers. I remember well the day when we were first shown an acacia, and the wood in which we were taught to know a wych-elm.

It was at Fockbury, during the holidays, after our father's second marriage, that under Alfred's leading, or 'orders' perhaps one might say, we began to act plays and eventually to write them. Some time in the day he would inform us that in the evening we were going to do a play, and thereupon would tell us the plot and assign to each of us our part; the dialogue, except for a few choice bits with which he supplied us, we had to invent for ourselves, and very badly we did it. Then,

(top)   FOCKBURY HOUSE (NEAR BROMSGROVE)
(bottom) PERRY HALL, BROMSGROVE

when our elders had dined – without any previous rehearsal, so far as I can remember – we gave our performance.

The plays, though they were Alfred's, were not good; such merits as they had were verbal, not dramatic; he stuffed us with a few jokes, keeping the best ones for himself, and in-between-whiles we carried on as best we could. From our elders we did not get much applause, nor did we deserve it; they were patient and acquiescent while we enjoyed ourselves. My clearest recollection is of a parody of Hamlet; the parody was Alfred's – Alfred was Hamlet. He entered sniffing and holding his nose, preliminary to his first remark, 'There's something rotting in the State of Denmark'. When he killed Polonius he cried, 'A rat, a rat, my kingdom for a rat!' That was about the quality of it; and as it came from him we considered it to be wit of the first order.

But when it came to serious play-writing (or what we regarded as serious), though Alfred lured us on to collaboration in a composite drama, he promised but did not perform. And for that reason 'the Tragedy of Lady Jane Grey', in which he was to have created the character of 'Bloody Queen Mary', remained unfinished, and the only good that came out of it was a song which he supplied to the writer of the scene where Lady Jane in captivity is nobly awaiting death. Of this early effort he thought sufficiently well to allow me to publish it in my reminiscences; so I give it here also.

Breathe, my lute, beneath my fingers
   One regretful breath,
One lament for life that lingers
   Round the doors of death.
For the frost has killed the rose,
And our summer dies in snows,
   And our morning once for all
   Gathers to the evenfall.

Hush, my lute, return to sleeping,
   Sing no songs again.
For the reaper stays his reaping
   On the darkened plain;
And the day has drained its cup,
And the twilight cometh up;
   Song and sorrow all that are
   Slumber at the even-star.

COLLEGE, AND LAST YEARS AT HOME

Having gained an open scholarship at St. John's
College, Oxford, in 1877, he went up in the autumn of
that year. There was no particular reason, except the
need for a good scholarship, why that college should have
been chosen. Unfortunately, his father would not allow
him to try for a Balliol Scholarship from disapproval of the
theological views of Dr. Jowett, the Master, nor did he wish
him to go to Cambridge unless he could obtain a scholarship at the college (St. John's) where uncles and grand-

parents had graduated, and where one had become Senior Dean. His Headmaster also was against Cambridge, saying that his English was not good enough.

It is probable that Cambridge, with its Classical Tripos, would have opened for him a better course of study than Oxford, where after gaining a First in Moderations in 1879, he failed in Greats two years later, so bringing his University career to a catastrophic end, which, for the time at any rate, destroyed all chance of a scholastic appointment at Oxford or Cambridge, and compelled him to take as an alternative the uncongenial work of a civil servant in H.M. Patent Office, where he remained for ten years.

Whatever the cause of his failure in Greats (for which some have been inclined to blame not him, but the examiners), Alfred said quite definitely in later years that the examiners had no alternative to the course they took. But to the best of my recollection, for home consumption (where the disappointment was naturally very great) he gave no explanation at all.

But though his Oxford career ended in failure he started it in good spirits, full of interest in his new surroundings, and his letters home during his first two years were long and amusing.

The following letter addressed to his stepmother is undated; it describes the opening of term in the autumn of 1877, and is probably the first that he wrote after entering College:

St. John's Coll.

Sunday.

... The ceremony of matriculation, which you want to hear about, was as follows. At a quarter to five on the Saturday afternoon all the freshmen of this college, twenty-two in number, were collected in Mr. Ewing's rooms, and were there instructed how to write our names in Latin in the Vice-Chancellor's books. Alfred, he said, became Alfredus, Edward, Edwardus, and so on; the surnames of course remaining unchanged. Then he marched us off to New College, where we found the Vice-Chancellor seated in dim religious light at the top of the hall. Another college was just concluding the ceremony, and when they had finished, we one by one inscribed our names in a large book, in this wise. 'Alfredus Edwardus Housman, e Coll. Di. Joh. Bapt. Gen. Fil. Natu max.' which is, being interpreted, 'A. E. Housman, of the College of St. John the Baptist, eldest son of a gentleman.' Sons of Clergymen write 'Cler. Fil' and sons of officers write 'Arm. Fil.' Then I wrote my name in English in a smaller and less dignified book, and then paid £2 10s. to a man at the table, and then we sat down one by one in a row till all had written their names and paid their fee. Then an attendant brought in twenty-two copies of the Statutes of the University, bound in violet, and piled them on the table, hiding the Vice-Chancellor from the eye. Presently his head appeared over the top, and we got up and stood in a sort of semi-circle in front of him. Then he called up each of us by name and presented each with a copy of the Statutes, and with a paper on which was written in Latin, or what passes for Latin at Oxford:

'At Oxford, in the Michaelmas term. A.D. 1877, on the 13th day of the month of October: on which day Alfred Edward Housman of the college of St. John the Baptist, gentleman's son, appeared in my presence, and was admonished to keep the laws of this University, and was enrolled in the register (Matricula) of the University

J. E. SEWELL
Vice-Chancellor'

Then he settled his gown over his shoulders and said 'Gentlemen of St. John's College, attend to me'. We attended. He said, in Latin, 'Allow me to inform you that you have this day been enrolled in the register of the University, and that you are bound to keep all the statutes contained in this book' (with the violet cover) 'as far as they may concern you.' Then we went. As to keeping the statutes contained in the violet cover, you may judge what a farce that is, when I tell you that you are forbidden to wear any coat save a black one, or to use fire-arms, or to trundle a hoop, among other things.

I went to Mr. Warren at Magdalen yesterday. I am going to him three times a week. Then I have nine lectures a week in college besides. Two men have invited me to breakfast next week, and Mr. Ewing has asked me to tea today along with several others, apropos of some Sunday-Night Essays, which are read by him and others in his rooms, and at which he invites us to attend. . . .

I hear that the gale did dreadful damage at the school. I am very glad that we suffered so comparatively little. I was afraid those beeches in the orchard would go. . . .

The following letter came later:

29 Nov. 1877

. . . This afternoon Ruskin gave us a great outburst against modern times. He had got a picture of Turner's, framed, and glassed, representing Leicester and the Abbey in the distance at Sunset, over a river. He read the account of Wolsey's death out of *Henry VIII*. Then he pointed to the picture as representing Leicester when Turner had drawn it. Then he said 'You, if you like, may go to Leicester to see what it is like now. I never shall. But I can make a pretty good guess.' Then he caught up a paintbrush. 'These stepping-stones of course have been done away with, and are replaced by a be-au-ti-ful iron bridge.' Then he dashed in the iron bridge on the glass of the picture. 'The colour of the stream is supplied on one side by the indigo factory.' Forthwith one side of the stream became indigo. 'On the other by the soap factory.' Soap dashed in. 'They mix in the middle – like curds,' he said, working them together with a sort of malicious deliberation. 'This field, over which you see the sun setting behind the abbey, is now occupied in a *proper* manner.' Then there went a flame of scarlet across the picture, which developed itself into windows and roofs and red brick, and rushed up into a chimney. 'The atmosphere is supplied – thus!' A puff and cloud of smoke all over Turner's sky: and then the brush thrown down, and Ruskin confronting modern civilization amidst a tempest of applause, which he always elicits now, as he has this term become immensely popular, his lectures being crowded, whereas of old he used to prophesy to empty benches. How he confuted the geological survey, and science in general, by the help of the college cook I have no time to tell you. . . .

Similar letters followed, but nowhere did he make mention of what proved to be one of the most important events in his life – the beginning of his great friendship with a fellow-scholar of St. John's, Moses Jackson, a man of brilliant scholastic attainment, though not a classic, and also a fine athlete. Dr. Alfred W. Pollard, a college friend of both, describes Jackson as 'an absolutely safe first in science' – who had therefore no need to read much in the evening. And it may well be that Alfred's close association with one who found study so little necessary may eventually have diverted him from his own book-work when studying for Greats. In any case he began soon to take an independent line, studying those classics which most interested him ('Propertius as a recreation', says Dr. Pollard), but with sufficient attention to the set course to secure an easy first in Mods.; perhaps it was secured too easily, so that he went on with undue confidence to his fall in Greats.

Political affairs also interested him; he had become a member of the Union, and in his second term he wrote to his father the following account of a debate on the burning question of the day, his own attitude over the matter being then, as always, whole-heartedly anti-Gladstone and pro-Beaconsfield:

February 12th, 1878.

Last Thursday a motion was brought on at the Union, to the following effect. 'That the Eastern policy of Lord Beaconsfield has been from the first, and remains utterly unworthy of the confidence of the country.' This was moved by a Balliol Liberal. Mr. Gladstone had been in Oxford a few days before, and a meeting was held at the Corn Exchange, where Mr. Gladstone spoke, and, I believe, moved some motion or other. A good many undergraduates in the hall held up their hands against this motion. Some of them were turned out, but I suppose Mr. Gladstone was disconcerted, for thereupon uprose Thorold Rogers, who holds, or rather has just vacated, the Professorship of Political Economy, and can therefore perhaps be scarcely held accountable for his actions, – he rose from Mr. Gladstone's side, and bade the rt. hon. gentleman be of good cheer, and pay no attention to 'dissipated undergraduates'. Now undergraduate Oxford was rather riled at this, and Professor

Thorold Rogers, who goes by the name of the Beaumont Street Gorilla, was considerably groaned for at the anti-Russian demonstration last Saturday, of which more anon, – and on Thursday, this opprobrious epithet was rankling in our hearts, and most were disposed to do anything to spite W.E.G. Owing to the excited state of the public mind, the attendance at the debate was tremendous: and then at the last moment before it began came those telegrams that the Russians were in Constantinople, and that Mr. Forster had withdrawn his amendment. The crush and the frantic excitement were such as the oldest inhabitant &c. The debate began with most of the House perpendicular, and some floating off their legs. Private business was got through in speed and silence; and then the terms of the motion were read. Then ensued seven good minutes of storm and tempest, and the cheering and groaning were such that neither could roar down the other, and they ceased from pure exhaustion. Then the speech began. It was not violent, which was a mercy, and not rhetorical, which was a greater mercy still. The man was nothing of the orator, but he was fluent, and very cool and impudent. The speech lasted an hour, but the greater part of this time was occupied by the speaking of the House, and not of the honourable member. I should not say that his remarks took more than twenty minutes, but they only cropped up as islets in the oceanic demonstration of opinion. About the middle of the speech, chairs were set on the dais usually reserved for the speakers; then the back ranks

45

made a rush forward, and more pressed in at the door: the poor new president was always on his legs to maintain order, and only the orator's head could be seen, which occasioned suggestions that he should stand on the table: – rejected, however, as savouring of stump oratory. There came then three other speakers, one for the motion and two against; the two were baldly bad, and the one was gaudily bad. Perhaps the one bye-cause of the great throng was the belief that Baumann, who is the best Union speaker, a Conservative, was going to speak. But he did not: the crowd diminished a little after the third speech: then, after the fourth speech, came the only glimmer of light in the darkness of debate: Burrows, the popular buffoon. He was better than I have heard him. It was rather ludicrous to hear him say that this was not the first time it had been his duty to vindicate Lord Beaconsfield's character, and that he hoped it would not be the last. Not that he did, in reality, vindicate it at all. He merely stated that Lord Beaconsfield's fame was a thing that would come – and come – and come, – when the honourable mover was gone – and gone – and gone. He then said that the honourable mover would rot. We must all rot. He did not, however, anticipate any precipitate action in that direction on the part of the honourable mover. Etc. etc. – sometimes slightly coarse, as you see, and sometimes really slightly witty. Then there came a priest from Keble, with an amendment which was precisely the same as the motion. He was a Liberal. Then a Conservative priest from Christ Church, in reply: then vociferations for a division. But there were several more speakers all the same. Then it was half-past eleven. Then someone proposed the adjournment of the debate, and someone else seconded it. The President stated that twelve honourable members had informed him they wished to speak on the question, and that some of them had left the House in anticipation of the adjournment of the debate. This struck us as highly insolent on their part, and we determined to serve them out by refusing to adjourn, especially as we had our majority on the spot. The last straw was laid on the camel's back by Lord Lymington, an Ex-president, who stated that he wanted to speak. His oratory is generally considered the one thing worse than death, and so the adjournment was negatived by a vast majority. The amendment was lost without a division. The division on the motion was – for the motion 68; against the motion 146, – majority against the motion unheard in the transports of enthusiasm, and the general rush back to college; for you can only understand the patriotic state of excitement in which we were, when you consider that the division took place between ten and five minutes to twelve: and if you are not back in college by 12, the penalties, I believe, are something very fearful indeed.

I did not go to Gladstone: I did not discover he was in Oxford till the moment before. He was rather feeble, as he tried to be humorous, which was very unwise. I believe he was very fine at the Palmerston

Club, in the passage where he described his antagonism to Lord Beaconsfield.

On Saturday night an anti-Russian demonstration was held in the Corn Exchange. I went, because Sir Robert Peel was coming: he did not come; but I heard Alfred Austin. The hall was crammed. The orators were late. First Rule Britannia was sung by the crowd; latent English Liberalism testified by scattered hisses its decided objection to the marine rule of Britannia. Then we took up our parable and sang that we didn't want to fight, but by jingo, if we did, we'd got the ships, we'd got the men, we'd got the money too. As a matter of fact we had not got the money yet, but that was immaterial; and growing impatience soon made it clear, by several 'mills' in the body of the hall, that when we *did* want to fight we could perfectly well dispense with money, and ships too, for the matter of that, in the attainment of our desire. When it was getting towards eight, the orators came. Then there was great cheering, and the Mayor was unheard, and Mr. Hall, member for the City of Oxford, (along with Sir William Harcourt!) began to speak . . . He said nothing worth remark, except that the Christians of Turkey hated one another with a hatred passing the love of women. This I relished very much, especially as his wife was sitting beside him. Then came Sir Henry Drummond Wolff, weak; then Mr. Hanbury, frantic, but gentlemanly: then Alfred Austin, pointed and clever, but insufficiently audible. These speeches formed the interludes to about a dozen patriotic ejections ... the result was rather a rowdy meeting. The motion – Conservative Turk – was of course carried with acclamation, and then the meeting fought itself out of doors and culminated in the combustion of an effigy of Mr. Gladstone just outside our college.

On the Sunday before last, Canon King, of Christ Church, preached at St. Mary's on "binding and loosing" – a counterblast to Dean Stanley in the *Nineteenth Century*. The sermon was unconscionably long, and considerably over our heads, brimming as it did with patristic learning, until, at the end of an hour and a quarter, he concluded with an apology to his younger brethren for having bored them, and giving as his reason that Our Lord grieved Peter, which I did not quite see the force of. But I felt it was quite worth sitting still for an hour and a quarter, to watch such an interesting personality. He is tall, but stoops; and haggard in the face but without grey hair; and his sermon was most masterly here and there. The exquisitely deprecating way and affected timidity with which he put his strongest points, and the mournful and apologetic modulation of his voice where he was pulling Dean Stanley to pieces, were really almost worthy of Disraeli, and not altogether unlike, were it not for the deadly earnest, which was rather detrimental to the oratorical effect.

Last Sunday, Dean Church in the morning. Dean Church, I regret to say it, is dull. He is very nice to look at, and particularly ethereal in countenance, and he

speaks in earnest, but he is certainly tedious. I thought
so last term, and now I am confirmed. In the afternoon,
the Bishop of Manchester, who commenced operations by
blowing his nose, which is a rhetorical device he has
apparently just found out, and which in the first ecstasy
of novelty he uses with injudicious profusion. In the
bidding prayer he prayed that this country might not
be drawn into war. He took a text to the effect that when
we saw devils being cast out, the kingdom of God would
be at hand. As he went on it became apparent that the
first Devil was the Turk. The second devil was the Pope,
over whose death-bed the Bishop uttered a wild whoop
of triumph, and then proceeded to inveigh against
the Romish Church, which inspired him with much
despair, as it did not seem inclined to die. This part of
the sermon was garnished with several quotations from
Macaulay's essay on Von Ranke's history of the Popes.
Now Canon Liddon was present, and up to this point
of course he must have found himself in unexpected
sympathy with the Bishop, – on both the Turk, and
Rome . . . Well, the Bishop, having shown us a great
deal of reason why the Church of Rome was unlikely to
go down quick into the pit, now began to give us a few
slight crumbs of consolation, on which we might base
a hope, though not a belief, that she would do so.
And then he somehow got upon the subject of Ritualism
and the Confessional in England.

Poor Canon Liddon! He always sits with his hand over
his face, so I could not see his emotions; but the revulsion

of feeling must have been great, when the sermon which began so promisingly, developed into this. But the Bishop was now far above Canons and all the rest of the inferior clergy. He began to plunge into eloquence, in which he rather staggered. He even began a sentence with 'Methinks' – but got rather bewildered towards the end of it, and so found it time to conclude with a remark about freedom of conscience, which was calculated to bring down the house, and then blew his nose in the middle of the doxology or whatever you call it, to show how little trouble it had all cost him. . . .

The next letter, addressed to his stepmother, refers to the famous by-election in which Sir William Harcourt, appointed Chancellor of the Exchequer in the new Gladstone Ministry, was defeated by his Conservative opponent, Mr. A. W. Hall.

May 10th, 1880

. . . You have seen by now that the strife is o'er, the battle done, the triumph, etc. Last week of course has been a scene of great excitement: the Campaign opened by the Vice-Chancellor announcing that any undergrad who should take part in any political meeting would be fined £5, which was gall and wormwood to a pretty large number of Liberals especially, who had been promising themselves the honour and glory of standing by Sir William Harcourt on the platform and spreading the wings of the University over him: Conservative under-graduates were less hard hit, as they none of them can speak decently. Hall himself, however, is an under-graduate, the senior undergraduate of Exeter; whether they have fined him £5 I can't say. We had great fun with Mr. Ewing who is one of the pro-Proctors this year; we told him we knew of an undergraduate who had spoken at every Conservative meeting during the Election, which wrought him up to wild excitement till we mentioned the name Alexander William Hall, after which his ardour seemed to cool . . . On Friday they were chairing Harcourt from the station to a mass-meeting at the Martyrs' Memorial, just outside College; we kept shouting out of the front windows Hurrah for Hall, at which the crowd looked up and made the scathing rejoinder – 'Yah! yer ain't got no votes!' which I daresay, however, was just as true for them as for us. On Saturday (election day) both the Candidates were driving about all over the town. Hall had got his infant sons in an open carriage with him, by way of appealing to the feelings. About midday, there came out a flaming poster in the Liberal colour (red) announcing that 'Frank Hedges had been detected endeavouring to record his vote twice, and was now in custody'. This I believe was true: But there instantly came out a blue placard that 'Frank Hedges had *not* recorded his vote twice and was now pursuing his ordinary avocations', which was also true, as Frank Hedges, whoever he may be, had of course only *tried* to record his vote twice, and had since been bailed off. At about a quarter to seven the poll was declared with a Conservative majority of 54, and immediately afterwards the numerous spectators crowded round the front of the Roebuck, Hall's head-quarters, observed an exciting scene. This was Mr. Hall at the centre window endeavouring to burst on to the balcony, and restrained by arm after arm thrown round his chest by his committee-men who dare not let him speak a word in that state of excitement. At intervals you saw him saying 'I *will* speak to them!' and breaking from his keepers halfway out of the window, and then he would be overwhelmed again and disappear. Finally one of his committee came out instead: this Gentleman's eloquence was confined to taking off his hat and whirling it round his head, and directing frightful grimaces of scorn and derision at the Randolph where Sir William Harcourt was. That evening we were forbidden to leave college after seven: and we were also forbidden to look out of the windows or in any way attract the attention of the mob; however, we blew horns out of the windows in great profusion, and on one of the dons coming round to demand the offending instrument he was presented with an aged and decrepit horn which had no inside and would not blow: so that in the morning he restored it with an apology, saying that he thought he must have made a mistake, as he could not make it give out any sound at all. We heard Sir William Harcourt booming away from the Randolph opposite, and he drove off for the first train with a body-guard of six policemen but we could not make out what he said; he said, however, that he bore no ill-feeling,

&c. &c.; so I suppose there will not be a petition, though of course this morning everyone is talking about bribery, just as I believe they did after the last Election. . . .

I give these letters at greater length than their intrinsic merit deserves, as being examples of a thoroughly cheerful amusement in men and things which never found such full expression afterwards. The one which is perhaps thoroughly worthy of the writer is that which describes Ruskin while lecturing. He told me, I remember, that Ruskin had a queer way of lifting his coat by the lapels while he talked and peeping bird-like down each sleeve in turn, and that his audience used to wait hungrily for him to break away from his script (which was sometimes dull in the manner of its delivery) into extempore passages that were wholly delightful and moving.

But Alfred was never one of the Master's followers; he regarded him rather as a curiosity of literature whose manners were charming but whose meaning was negligible.

In his second term Alfred entered for the Hertford Scholarship and was one of the first six: 'Which', he wrote, 'is better than anyone else thought I should do, and better than I myself fancied I had actually done.'

His attempt for the Newdigate Prize in 1879, on the set subject of Iona, had little merit; it was indeed less good than his two last school prize-poems. He sat up all one night writing it, and in College chapel the next morning heard read the sentence: 'We have toiled all the night and have taken nothing', which he applied, truly enough, to his own useless labour.

Early in 1878, he contributed, under a pseudonym, to a magazine run by undergraduates, which lived for rather less than a year. When he was telling me in later days what I might or might not publish of his early writings, I reminded him of these. There was no question of my wish to republish them, but when I asked whether I might reveal the pseudonym under which he had written, 'I should be very much obliged to you', he said, 'if you would not'. He agreed that these later pieces were less good than what he had produced so easily for home consumption, because, he said, the latter were done to meet Editor's need of copy, the other spontaneously for mere amusement.

But even while he was thoroughly enjoying himself during those first two years at Oxford, the underlying streak of shadow was there waiting to extend itself over a mind and temperament singularly prone to melancholy when circumstances became adverse. It is significant that the only two pictures which he bought to embellish his College rooms were Dürer's 'Melancholia' and 'The Knight, Death, and the Devil'; and except for group-photographs of College teams, in which his friend Jackson figured along with others, he brought nothing else back with him from Oxford in the way of pictures. When he finally came down in 1881 after his failure in Greats, all hope of an immediate academic career was over. He returned to Oxford for one term to read for a pass degree in classics, but wasted no money in taking up the degree until he was appointed to be Professor of Latin at University College, London. His academic failure was not the only shadow which fell upon his life at that time: there were others, financial and personal.

In a letter to a friend two years before his death, when the increasing disabilities of age were troubling him, 'My life is bearable,' he wrote, 'but I do not want to continue it, and I wish it had ended a year and a half ago. The great and real troubles of my early manhood did not render those days so permanently unsatisfactory as these.'

THE HEAVY CHANGE

In the autobiographical note from which I have already quoted: 'Oxford', wrote Alfred, 'had not much effect on me, except that I there met my greatest friend.' A statement which can hardly be as true as he would have liked it to be, since this, at any rate, can be said for certain.– he came back from Oxford a changed character. It was probably the blow of his failure which caused him to withdraw completely into himself, and become a silent and impenetrable recluse in the midst of his own family during the eighteen months which elapsed before he left home to take up his Civil Service appointment in London.

Up to the beginning of his University career he had been, as I have already told, our social and intellectual

A. E. HOUSMAN
AGED 18

leader, the instigator of all our attempts in prose and poetry. When he came back, and for a good many years afterwards, we ceased to know him – mainly, if not entirely, because he was determined not to be known. If sympathy was what he feared to receive on his return from Oxford, he took the best means to deprive himself of it; and only very occasionally at first, then gradually as the years went on, did he allow a breaking-down of the barrier.

During those first years at Oxford, his correspondence with members of the family had been lively and amusing; so also during vacation there was no diminution of his social affability. During one summer vacation he brought his college friend A. W. Pollard to stay with us. And this proved the beginning of a new and enduring friendship for other members of the family, for which I especially have reason to be grateful. It must have been during those intervals of college life that Alfred delighted us with some of his best pieces of nonsense verse. Our evening diversions, almost as long as I can remember, had often been of a semi-literary character. One of these was the writing of short poems, containing a collection of nouns, each member of the company supplying one. Here is a sample of the sort of thing which Alfred was able to turn out in the course of fifteen or twenty minutes. The nouns were: hat, novel, banker, cucumber, yacht, and abridgment. Obviously the last was the crux; and this is how Alfred tackled it:

At the door of my own little hovel,
Reading a novel I sat;
And as I was reading the novel
A gnat flew away with my hat.
As fast as a fraudulent banker
Away with my hat it fled,
And calmly came to an anchor
In the midst of the cucumber-bed.

I went and purchased a yacht,
And traversed the garden-tank,
And I gave it that insect hot
When I got to the other bank;
Of its life I made an abridgment
By squeezing it somewhat flat,
And I cannot think what that midge meant
By flying away with my hat.

One Christmas (1879, I think), we attempted something more ambitious, which produced a memorable result. Each wrote a story, and on Christmas Eve, or thereabouts, the stories were read out to the assembled family. Alfred's contribution was a domestic sketch in verse and prose entitled 'A Morning with the Royal Family', the opening sentence of which ran: ' "Pigs on the front lawn again!" cried the King, "Give me a cannon, somebody!" Nobody gave him a cannon, so seizing a tea-spoon from the breakfast-table he rushed from the apartment.' This is the story – the only complete work of fiction, I think, which he ever produced – which was published a year or two later, without his permission, in the Bromsgrove School Magazine, and has remained ever since a prized but rather private family possession, re-publication having been strictly forbidden by the author.

In the school it had a great success—even the Headmaster enjoyed it; but it contained two improprieties of a profane character – or what were thought to be so in those days; and, in order that none might be scandalized, the Head-master caused little slips of paper to be pasted over the offending words, with harmless substitutes printed thereon. Of course, they were all picked away in no time, but the symbolic fig-leaves served their purpose, indicating a belated censorship for the satisfaction of school parents.[1]

Alfred's indulgence in nonsense verse remained fairly continuous even during the dry years between his de-parture from Oxford and his first publication of poems. When the Salvation Army was becoming a prominent movement, he wrote and sent the following to a member of his family:

'Hallelujah!' was the only observation
That escaped Lieutenant-Colonel Mary Jane,
When she tumbled off the platform in the station,
And was cut in little pieces by the train.
  Mary Jane, the train is through yer:
  Hallelujah, Hallelujah!
We will gather up the fragments that remain.

[1] Of what untold rarity must any copy be which still contains the fig-leaves! Collectors had better make a note.

These verses were actually written when word reached him that I had just published a book of devotional poems: then, writing to our stepmother, he said that he had thoughts of doing something of the same kind himself, and these lines were enclosed as one of two samples.

Several other poems, which he did not release till later, were written during the same period, but it was not till after his appointment in 1892 as Professor of Latin at University College, London, that he began once more to allow his nonsense verses free circulation, and probably also to write them more often.

The years during which he kept himself most apart from his family were those which he spent as a Civil Service clerk at the Patent Office (1882-92): and though for nearly the whole of that time two of us were living in London, and though he would come dutifully to see us whenever invited, he never asked us to his own rooms in return.

This was his Purgatory period: it started with his quittance of Oxford, and only ended when he became Professor of Latin at University College, London.

During the months when he had to remain at home, preparing for the examination which he must pass for entry into the Civil Service, we had daily before our eyes an amazing example of his power of concentration. The dining-room was the most available room in the house (with a fire) where he could work; and as this was the room in which a good deal of the household activities went on, with constant comings and goings of various members of the family, and sometimes with conversation added, he had to share it and put up with the general household arrangements. Into this room, as soon as breakfast had been cleared, Alfred would bring his books, and sitting at the table would study for the whole morning, oblivious apparently to what went on around him. But was he? Was it not more likely an exasperating strain on his powers of endurance, which he controlled with an iron will?

While at home he got some temporary employment from his old Headmaster in teaching the Sixth Form Greek and Latin, and earned thereby a testimonial which was useful ten years later, stating that he had proved himself a thorough and sympathetic teacher, warmly interested in his work and his pupils.

For the first few years of his life in London on taking up his appointment at the Patent Office, he shared rooms in Bayswater with his friend Moses Jackson, and a younger brother named Adalbert, whose death some years later is commemorated in the verses which appear in *More Poems* under the initials A.J.J. In Alfred's rooms at Trinity College, Cambridge, the portraits of these two brothers hung near together over the fireplace – the one a portrait taken in youth, the other in late middle-age. One day, looking at the latter, I asked Alfred who he was. In a strangely moved voice he answered, 'That was my friend Jackson, the man who had more influence on my life than anybody else.' This closest of all his friends died in Vancouver in 1923; and on going through my brother's correspondence after his death, I found an envelope endorsed, 'Mo's last letter'. The letter had been written faintly in pencil, in the hospital where Jackson died soon after; and above the faint writing, the better to preserve it (keeping the form of each word carefully), Alfred had himself gone over the whole in ink.

To the rooms which he was sharing with his two friends when my sister Clemence and I started our life in London, Alfred asked us not to come; and we only met Jackson once by accident at the house of a mutual friend, when he seemed surprised to find that Alfred had a brother and sister living near him. This shows how rigidly at that time Alfred was keeping his family at a distance. Nevertheless, he came to see us when we asked him, but our relations remained for some years strained and perfunctory.

But when, a year or two later, he went to live alone at Byron Cottage, Highgate, and asked our stepmother, who was then visiting us, to come and see him, he told me that I might come too; and being of a forgiving disposition I did so.

A curious little incident, characteristic of both, marked that visit. 'The Mater' was anxious to see what sort of a landlady Alfred had to look after him, and asked that she should be sent up for inspection. Alfred flatly refused: his landlady was not to be made a show. The Mater, as we came away, seemed puzzled, and also a little suspicious, though I thought Alfred's objection reasonable; but as it would have required too much explanation to make her see it, I did not try to explain.

Of that same landlady he told us, shortly after the publication of *A Shropshire Lad,* an amusing story. She was about to engage a new cook, and finding one of the applicants satisfactory was preparing to conclude terms, when the question was unexpectedly put to her whether she had a poet on the premises. The landlady, in all good faith, assured her that she had not. It then appeared that in her last place there were *two* poets – one a Mr. Swinburne, the other a Mr. Watts-Dunton. ('I am sure', said Alfred in parenthesis, 'that Watts-Dunton must have told her that himself, for nobody else could have done so.') Further explanation followed: she said that when either of these poets felt like writing a poem, they required a savoury as a necessary stimulant; and as inspiration generally came at about two o'clock in the morning, she was constantly being called out of her bed to bring poetry to the birth. Hence her precautionary inquiry whether, in her new place, there were any poets; she was not going to let it happen again.

I have a suspicion that this story got embellished in the telling, and that Alfred passed it on largely for the pleasure of saying what he thought about the poetry of Mr. Watts-Dunton, in a connection which enabled him to say lightly what he would not have troubled to say seriously.

RETURN TO ACADEMIC LIFE

It was, perhaps, as an indication that the reasons for proud seclusion were over, that he invited me to hear him give his Introductory Lecture at University College, London, on October 3rd, 1892, soon after his appointment as Latin Professor; and I then had the amusement of hearing the shocked 'Tut-tuts' with which some of the students greeted his slighting reference to the utilitarian view of education taken by Mr. Herbert Spencer, who was more highly thought of in those days than he is now, but who had always been A.E.H.'s particular *bête noire*. One of his College friends told me that when at Oxford he was already casting scorn on Spencer's claim to be regarded either as a philosopher or a thinker deserving of respect. I do not know how he would have taken the information which has recently come to us that Herbert Spencer was, through our Brettell relations, a connection of the family. It appears also that for two years in his early days Spencer lived at Bromsgrove as a civil engineer in the employ of the London and Birmingham Railway Co.; but that was long before our time.

I quote here the concluding passage of the Introductory Lecture, as summarizing briefly my brother's estimate of the special value of knowledge, which was his main thesis:

'It is the glory of God, says Solomon, to conceal a thing: but the honour of kings is to search out a matter.

Kings have long abdicated that province; and we students are come into their inheritance: it is our honour to search out the things which God has concealed. In Germany at Easter time they hide coloured eggs about the house and the garden that the children may amuse themselves in hunting after them and finding them. It is to some such game of hide-and-seek that we are invited by that power which planted in us the desire to find out what is concealed, and stored the universe with hidden things that we might delight ourselves in discovering them. And the pleasure of discovery differs from other pleasures in this, that it is shadowed by no fear of satiety on the one hand or of frustration on the other. Other desires perish in their gratification, but the desire of knowledge never: the eye is not satisfied with seeing nor the ear filled with hearing. Other desires become the occasion of pain through dearth of the material to gratify them, but not the desire of knowledge: the sum of things to be known is inexhaustible, and however long we read we shall never come to the end of our story-book. So long as the mind of man is what it is, it will continue to exult in advancing on the unknown throughout the infinite field of the universe; and the tree of knowledge will remain for ever, as it was in the beginning, a tree to be desired to make one wise.'

While at University College, Alfred contributed occasional nonsense rhymes to the *Union Magazine*, three of which (though not his best) he allowed to be privately reprinted in 1935. I should therefore feel at liberty to include them in my own selection; but as I have better ones to offer (especially a much finer version of the Amphisbaena poem), I leave them to the safe keeping of the Department of English, University College, London, where searchers for curios may find them.

He also gave, on eight occasions, a written paper on one of the British poets, before the College Literary Society; his chosen poets were Tennyson, Matthew Arnold, Burns, Campbell, Erasmus Darwin, Swinburne, and 'The Spasmodic School'. He was only quite kind to two of them – Matthew Arnold and Campbell; all the others were subjected to varying degrees of satirical criticism – so severe, in the case of Burns, that a Scottish professor, touched to his native quick (or pretending to be), declared in the discussion which followed that forgiveness was the last refuge of malignity: he would not forgive Professor Housman. But there was no real wrath in him; Alfred's gibes did no harm to friends who understood him.

As A.E.H. has left a very strict injunction that these papers, together with all his other prose manuscripts in whatever language, are to be destroyed, and as I have been taken to task by certain loose-minded critics for my obedience, I had better say something about them. In the first place, had A.E.H. doubted my respect for his wishes over a matter which he had every right to decide, he would, I feel sure, have destroyed not merely the papers but everything else – poems as well as prose. His reliance on my sense of duty toward him has therefore saved those at any rate.

Then, as to the literary value of the papers themselves. Nobody can take a greater delight in the wit and subtle malevolence of my brother's critical writings than I do; but I believe he was right in not wishing that these somewhat casual compositions should remain to have their defects and occasional unfairnesses regarded as representative of his real and well-considered literary judgments. They were written, not as a sequence, to amuse, stimulate and occasionally exasperate an audience composed mostly of young people; and they had in them exaggerated statements which were sometimes very funny, but not always true. They were also very characteristic of his method of combining sharp sarcasm with generous praise wherever he thought either to be deserved. Having tumbled Tennyson somewhat roughly on the ground of his popularity, he set him on his throne again in a peroration which went so far as to declare that there was no English poet, except Shakespeare himself, who had produced excellent things so diverse in their excellence. And though in each case the praise finally awarded differed appropriately, he had equally handsome things to say of the poets whom, in earlier passages, he held up to something like ridicule.

Matthew Arnold he placed high: both as a critic and as an interpreter of human life in its relation to the Powers Above. This was an opinion which he had formed early: in his Oxford days he told a friend that for him, the long passage in 'Empedocles on Etna' which begins 'The out-spread world to span' contained all the law and the prophets (the law and the prophets, that is to say, as he himself read them). His final words on Arnold were to defend him from those who said that his poetry lacked emotion; and he gave as proof the poem, which was one of his own (A.E.H.'s) favourites, addressed to an unsuccessful soldier in the war of liberation of humanity,

> Creep into thy narrow bed,
> Creep, and let no more be said!
> Vain thy onset! all stands fast;
> Thou thyself must break at last.

In this, and in the three stanzas that follow, is a voice near in tone to the voice of *A Shropshire Lad*.

Of Burns he said that, though not a great poet, he was something rarer still, a great critic: a ground for praise which many warmer admirers of the poet would not perhaps have discovered. It was, generally a characteristic of each paper that there was more originality of criticism in the praise than in the blame.

In defining the merits of Swinburne – the vigour and magnificence of his verse – he used an interesting comparison from his appreciation of architecture. Henry the Seventh's chapel, he said, was not the most beautiful part of Westminster Abbey, but that part had a beauty which did more to enrich the whole by being itself new and different; and it was better to have that difference of a less pure style than a mere addition of the better thing. Swinburne, he said, was assuredly not the greatest English poet of the nineteenth century; but of the two most original, Swinburne was one, Wordsworth was the other.

These papers have to share the fate of a very much better one – the Inaugural Lecture which my brother gave on his appointment, in 1911, to the Kennedy Professorship of Latin at Cambridge University, and which he would not allow to be published because of his inability to retrace his authority for a statement which he had made concerning a Shelley manuscript, as to which later investigation has gone rather against him.

'Do not tell me', was his comment on another refusal to permit a certain publication, 'that there is much more vanity than modesty in this, because I know it already.' But if it were vanity it only arose from his rigid adherence to the high standard which he had set himself, with anything below which he did not wish to be identified.

The testimonials which secured him his appointment to the Professorship of Latin at London University were remarkable both for the eminence of their signatories in the world of scholarship, and for the manner in which their recipient had secured the recognition they accorded him. For here was a man whose University course had ended in failure; for ten years he had been separated from academic life; and only by having passed the examination required for becoming a B.A. had he kept the necessary connection with his University to enable him to take the degree of M.A. It was solely by his writings in the *Journal of Philology*, the *Classical Review*, and other learned publications, that he had established his reputation among the scholars not only of his own country, but of Europe and America. In his letter of application for the appointment was the admission of the remarkable fact which might have lost him the post: 'In 1881 I failed to obtain honours in the Final School of Literae Human-iores.'

Among the writers of the testimonials was Robinson Ellis, Professor of Latin at Oxford, one of the many whom, in matters of scholarship, A.E.H. subsequently handled somewhat severely. As an instance of the 'grooviness' of certain distinguished men of learning, I may here mention that when I met Professor Ellis in 1902, and, in answer to his question whether I were related to 'another Housman', whose Christian name he had forgotten, replied, 'You mean A.E., the author of *A Shropshire Lad*' – 'No, no,' he said, 'the man I mean is a Latin scholar.' *A Shropshire Lad* he had either never heard of, or did not know of the connection. The mistake more usually made at that time, and ever since until recently, was not a disconnection of A.E.H. the Latinist from A.E.H. the poet, but a confusion between A.E.H. and myself, about which Alfred had things to say which I shall presently quote.

LIFE IN LONDON

In the autobiographical note from which I have already quoted, Alfred writes of his years in London as follows:

'While I was at the Patent Office I read a great deal of Greek and Latin at the British Museum of an evening. While at University College, which is not residential, I lived alone in lodgings in the environs of London. *A Shropshire Lad* was written at Byron Cottage, 17 North Road, Highgate, where I lived from 1886 to 1905.

'*A Shropshire Lad* was offered to Macmillan, and declined by them on the advice, I have been told, of John Morley, who was their reader. Then a friend introduced me to Kegan Paul; but the book was published at my own expense.'

It was to this friend (Alfred W. Pollard) that he owed a change in the proposed title of the book, which must have had a considerable effect on its fortunes. He had intended to call it *Poems by Terence Hearsay*. Pollard suggested *A Shropshire Lad* as better, a piece of good advice which the author was luckily not above taking.

'The Shropshire Lad', the note goes on to say, 'is an imaginary figure, with something of my temper and view of life. Very little in the book is biographical.'

As regards the influences affecting his poems, he added: ' "Reader of the Greek Anthology" [which his correspondent had suggested] is not a good name for me. Of course I have read it, or as much of it as is worth reading, but with no special heed; and my favourite Greek poet is Aeschylus. No doubt I have unconsciously been influenced by the Greeks and Latins, but I was surprised when critics spoke of my poetry as "classical". Its chief sources of which I am conscious are Shakespeare's songs, the Scottish Border ballads, and Heine.'

In answer to an inquiry whether *A Shropshire Lad* had been the product of 'a crisis of pessimism' he replied that he had never had any such crisis. 'In the first place, I am not a pessimist but a pejorist (as George Eliot said she was not an optimist but a meliorist); and that is owing to my observation of the world, not to personal circumstances. Secondly, I did not begin to write poetry in earnest until the really emotional part of my life was over; and my poetry, so far as I could make out, sprang chiefly from physical conditions, such as a relaxed sore throat during my most prolific period, the first five months of 1895.'

Finally, to the same correspondent, he wrote: 'I respect the Epicureans more than the Stoics, but I am myself a Cyrenaic. Pascal and Leopardi I have studied with great admiration; Villon and Verlaine very little, Calderon and German philosophers not at all. For Hardy I felt affection, and high admiration for some of his novels and a few of his poems.

'As some of the questions which you ask in your flattering curiosity may be asked by future generations, and as many of them can only be answered by me, I make this reply.'

I should not have suspected Alfred of writing letters to the papers about anything; but I am told that he wrote six at least, and I found among his notes, after his death,

rough drafts of one or two (one written during the War)
which may or may not have been sent and published.
This that follows was of an earlier date, written, as the
contents indicate, while he was living at Highgate. It
was headed 'Highgate Wood', dated March 1894, and
was addressed to the Editor of the *Standard*:

SIR,

In August, 1886, Highgate Wood became the property
of the Mayor and Commonalty and Citizens of the City
of London. It was then in a very sad state. So thickly
was it overgrown with brushwood, that if you stood in
the centre you could not see the linen of the inhabitants
of Archway Road hanging to dry in their back gardens.
Nor could you see the advertisements of Juggins' stout
and porter which surmounts the front of the public house
at the south corner of the wood. Therefore the Mayor
and Commonalty and Citizens cut down the intervening
brushwood, and now when we stand in the centre we can
divide our attention between Juggins' porter and our
neighbour's washing. Scarlet flannel petticoats are much
worn in Archway Road, and if anyone desires to feast his
eyes on these very bright and picturesque objects, so
seldom seen in the streets, let him repair to the centre of
Highgate Wood.

Still we were not happy. The wood is bounded on the
north by the railway to Muswell Hill, and it was a common subject of complaint in Highgate that we could not
see the railway from the wood without going quite to

the edge. At length, however, the Mayor and Commonalty and Citizens have begun to fell the trees on the north, so that people in the centre of the wood will soon be able to look at the railway when they are tired of the porter and the petticoats. But there are a number of new red-brick houses on the east side of the wood, and I regret to say that I observe no clearing of timber in that direction. Surely, sir, a man who stands in the centre of the wood, and knows that there are new red-brick houses to the east of him, will not be happy till he sees them.

Sir, it is spring: birds are pairing, and the County Council has begun to carve the mud-pie which it made last year at the bottom of Waterlow Park. I do not know how to address the Mayor and Commonalty; but the Citizens of the City of London all read the *Standard*, and surely they will respond to my appeal and will not continue to screen from my yearning gaze any one of those objects of interest which one naturally desires to see when one goes to the centre of a wood.

I am, sir,

Your obedient servant,

A.E.H.

During the years preceding his appointment at University College, London, Alfred remained for most of the members of his family a somewhat distant acquaintance, and neither from our occasional meetings, nor from our quite formal correspondence, have I anything to record that seems now worth telling. Indeed, it was not until

after *A Shropshire Lad* was published that our correspondence became fairly frequent, and his letters
began once more to be individual and amusing. The
astonished exclamation of a member of the family, after
reading the first six or seven of the *Shropshire Lad*
poems, 'Alfred has a heart!' is sufficient indication of the
pains he had taken to conceal it during the years of his
bitter disappointment over the finish of his university
career. But even while he lived so far removed from the
familiar associations of early days, he still had his eye on
us, as regards our literary activities, and when any of
them pleased him, he let us know of it.

When his sister Clemence's story, *The Were Wolf*,
appeared in the Christmas number of *Atalanta* in the
late 'eighties, she got from him a letter of warm appreciation beginning 'Capital, capital, capital!' And quite
early, with my own stories, poems, and plays, I was
conscious of having more regard for what Alfred would
think and say of them than for what any other critic or
the general public might think or say; for which reason,
even when our relations were not intimate, I generally
sent to him for criticism all my books of verse before
publication; and because he took the trouble to read and
to suggest improvements, one of those books, *The Mother
Goose and her Seven Young Goslings*, has in it a couplet
of his own composing, in place of what he was kind
enough to say were the only two bad lines in the whole
poem. The couplet which he sent me and which I
gratefully accepted was this:

Entombed in a wolf was her husband the gander,
And the painful event had completely unmanned
her.

– a small but kindly bit of collaboration which greatly
pleased me.

It so happened that I sent him the manuscript of my
first book of poems for criticism, at the very time when,
without my knowing it, he was preparing his own for
publication; and I got from him two long letters of
detailed criticism – sometimes scathing in its terms, but
also considerate and kind where it seemed to him that
kindness was deserved.

Shortly after our two books had been published, I
received a letter from him, the terms of which will be
better understood if I explain beforehand that I had
designed for the cover of my own book, *Green Arras*, a
very elaborate, and, as I thought, beautiful cover of gold
scroll-work.

24 Dec. 1896

. . . I am extremely anxious that you should spend
a happy Christmas; and as I have it in my power, – here
goes. Last night at dinner I was sitting next to Rendall,
Principal of University College Liverpool and Professor
of Greek there, a very nice fellow and a great student of
Marcus Aurelius and modern poetry. He was interested
to hear that you were my brother: he said that he had
got *Green Arras*, and then he proceeded, 'I think it is

the best volume by him that I have seen: the *Shropshire Lad* had a pretty cover'.

I remain

Your affectionate brother (what a thing is fraternal affection, that it will stand these tests!)

A. E. Housman.

P.S. After all, it was I who designed that pretty cover; and he did not say that the cover of *Green Arras* was pretty. (*Nor is it.*)

P.P.S. I was just licking the envelope, when I thought of the following venomed dart: I had far, far rather that people should attribute my verses to you than yours to me.

This was the sort of thing which he enjoyed writing; and to me it was done less maliciously than to others, because he knew that I also enjoyed it, having reason to know that sometimes he said kinder things about me behind my back than he wrote to my face. But there can be no doubt that he did greatly enjoy writing and saying bitter and contemptuous things about people who seemed to him to deserve them; and he had in his note-book a whole stock of phrases which were apparently waiting till opportunity came for him to use them. This statement has been queried by a friend who thinks that so cold-blooded a preparation of gall and wormwood for future victims was unlikely, and that they were all written for an immediate occasion; but in the note-books I found five pages of them obviously awaiting application; and so long as he did not apply them until they were deserved, it was well, I think, that those happy thoughts should be jotted down for safe keeping, as they occurred to him. Some of them, but by no means all, found a place in his critical writings – one in an improved form in the Cambridge Inaugural Lecture of 1911, others in the introductions to his own editions of the classics, and in his periodical reviews of books by other scholars whose claim to that term he sometimes would not admit.

Our younger sister Katharine – known always as Kate – was the one of us who maintained the most permanent connection with Alfred throughout his life. The most amusing of his letters written from Oxford had been addressed to her, and were the beginning of a continuous correspondence that lasted as long as he lived. Her marriage in 1887 to E. W. Symons – once a Fellow of Alfred's own College at Oxford – opened to him a family life that he found both pleasant and interesting. His nephews' creditable careers gratified him; and he gave them generous assistance during the war, in which all four of them became engaged. Holiday companionship with his brother-in-law was agreeable to him, and helped him many times when he needed change from his work at Cambridge. He was a never-failing source of help to this sister in historical research which she carried on for many years in compiling a history of King Edward's School, Bath, of which her husband was Headmaster. It was his pleasure to make her a life member of the London Library in order to help her; and the letter in which he announced this benefaction is very characteristic of him:

Trinity College
Cambridge
15 Jan. 1926.

My Dear Kate,

I am obliged to write to you, as otherwise you may be perplexed by communications from the London Library. I am taking steps to have you made a life member: but as you cannot be selected before Feb. 8 (if then), the Librarian suggests sending you a receipt 'Subject to the Committee's Approval' which will entitle you to full privilege and enable you to make use of the Library at once in your own right. Finally you will have to sign a form. Make hay while the sun shines, for perhaps the Committee will not approve of you.

Your affectionate brother
A. E. Housman.

'SHROPSHIRE LAD' YEAR AND AFTER

When I am told that the author of *A Shropshire Lad* was of more pre-eminent rank as a scholar than as a poet, the information – though I have no doubt that it is true – leaves me unmoved in my own personal devotion. Exact scholarship is a rare and a high virtue; but to me it is a cold one; while the writing of even a single good poem secures for its author not merely my respect but my warm gratitude. And truly the day when I first opened *A Shropshire Lad* and found there more than thirty

79

very good poems awaiting me, was one of the great
events of my life.

Alfred had kept it a sealed secret from his family until
the day of publication; and though I had, by a chance
indiscretion, got wind of it from the publisher who was
also my publisher, its quality came on me like thunder
out of a clear sky. Before the end of the day I knew a
dozen of the poems by heart, and before the end of a
week nearly all of them; and my legs being then young,
capable of keeping pace with the enthusiasm of my
tongue, I ran around among my friends reciting those
which were already my favourites, and always, I think —
for my friends were of my own generation and literary
in their tastes — with acceptance. One friend, to whose
household I had sent a copy of the poems, flung open her
window to a London street as she saw me coming to the
door a week later, and cried rapturously: 'Oh, L.H., what
beautiful poems your brother has written!'

But the elder generation did not give them the same
welcome. Millington, Headmaster of Bromsgrove
School, to whom Alfred had sent a presentation copy, said
that the poems were not good. A few years ago, when I
quoted this to my brother, he said, 'Well, of course, the
only poetry that Millington was able to admire was
Tennyson's.' But even a college friend, to whom he had
submitted the poems for criticism before publication,
regarded as a fond extravagance my declaration that they
were better than Stevenson's *Underwoods* — R.L.S. being
then very much more the fashion than he is now. Mr.

Edmund Gosse, who had a weakness for suspecting any literary discoveries but his own, said sneeringly to a brother-critic: 'Who is this "house-boat" person they are all chattering about?' A week later, he had changed his tone, and was chattering himself in three whole columns, very appreciatively and well.

But though the literary world had become aware, within the first month of its appearance, that a new poet had arisen, only three hundred and eighty-one copies of the book had been sold, at half-a-crown each, by the end of the year; and two years after, finding that six copies of the first edition still remained unsold, I bought the lot, gave some away, and then thirty years later, after telling Alfred that I was going to have a ramp with the second-hand book-market, I contrived to sell one 'unopened' copy for £12, the next for £20, the next for £30, and the last, which he obligingly inscribed for me to make it unique, for £70. It sold later in America for £80, which I believe constitutes the top price up to date. Proud of my exploit, I wrote to Alfred offering him the proceeds as more rightfully belonging to him than to me. In his reply, ignoring my monetary offer, he wrote from Trinity College, Cambridge:

29 Dec. 1925

At our last Feast I had the new Dean of Westminster next me, and he said he had long been wanting to thank me for the amusement he had derived from my writings, especially about Queen Victoria and her ministers. So if I bring you money, you bring me fame.

This was not the only occasion on which we were mistaken for each other by people who ought to have known better. I was once introduced to an audience in his own school hall by the Headmaster of Westminster, as 'a classical scholar of European fame'. To avoid exposing his ignorance in the place of his authority, I bowed submissive to the compliment, though I had derisive friends in the audience who knew better.

It happened that, in the same year when *A Shropshire Lad* was published, I went to stay with friends at Buildwas; and finding that Hughley and its steeple were only five miles away, I walked over to have a look at the 'farknown sign' and the graves of suicides on the north side of the tower. When I reached it, I found that the 'farknown sign' was buried away in a valley, and that the suicides were most of them respectable church-wardens and wives of vicars, all in neatly-tended graves. When I reproached Alfred for his romantic falsification of local history, his explanation was that the place he really meant had an ugly name, so he substituted Hughley. 'I did not apprehend', he wrote, 'that the faithful would be making pilgrimages to these holy places.' But that is what has now happened. That small book of poems has given to many Shropshire place-names an added romance comparable to that which attaches to the place-names of Hardy's novels. But I wonder would that have happened had the poems been published under the title originally chosen for them.

It was, perhaps, when *Poems by Terence Hearsay* was

still the proposed title, that Mr. Blackett, one of the publishing directors, made suggestions with a view to securing popularity which Alfred felt obliged to turn down. About that and other points, shortly after the book was published, he wrote to me as follows:

Yes, the cover and title-page are my own. Blackett was very amusing. He was particularly captivated with the military element; so much so that he wanted me at first to make the whole affair, with Herbert's assistance, [Herbert being our youngest brother, who had himself enlisted] into a romance of enlistment. I had to tell him that this would probably take me another thirty-six years. Then the next thing was, he thought it would be well to have a design on the cover representing a yokel in a smock frock with a bunch of recruiting-sergeant's ribbons in his hat: this too I would not. Everything has its drawbacks, and the binding seems to me so extraordinarily beautiful that I cannot bear to lose sight of it by opening the book: when I take it down with the intention of reading it, the cover detains me in a stupor of admiration till it is time to go to bed.

It is interesting to know, in view of the many poems which he wrote about enlistment and fighting, that he regarded patriotism as a dangerous subject for poets. Of all the virtues, he said, the one which had inspired the least amount of good poetry was patriotism, the reason being that it so easily degenerated into vice,

83

for when poets began praising their own country they commonly ended by insulting others.

I have already said that the elder generation were not specially kind to the book on its first appearance; George Meredith, who received a copy from an enthusiastic friend, did not show much liking for it; 'an orgy of naturalism' was his description of it; and John Morley, as has been told, was responsible for its rejection by the publishers to whom it was first offered.

In America by the aid of pirate-editions, it received fairly soon an enthusiastic welcome. One young American poet, whom I met on my first visit to that country, told me that, after reading it, he lay awake all night weeping for joy. When I told Alfred this, he laughed, but I am sure it pleased him. So also did this story which I was able to pass on to him a few years ago. I had been giving a lecture – not on poetry; at the end a man came up to me and asked if I was the author of *A Shropshire Lad*. I said 'No'. 'Any relation?' 'Yes, I am his brother.' 'Ah, well,' was the kind reply, 'that's something to be proud of. I, too, have a brother who is the better man.'

HIS LIKINGS IN LITERATURE

Judging by the contents of Alfred's bookshelves, his tastes in English literature (so far as fiction was concerned) were by no means highbrow. He liked detective novels, and ghost stories – even poor ones apparently, which he

A. E. HOUSMAN
AGED 35

did not try to defend from my criticism, only saying that their writer, with whom he was friendly, had done better things of an earlier date. He liked American writers much better than he liked America, and claimed to have introduced *Gentlemen Prefer Blondes* to the English public by first popularizing it among the dons of Cambridge. It was he, in our early days, who introduced us to the delights of Louisa Alcott's *Little Women* and *Good Wives,* and Max Adeler's *Out of the Hurly-Burly.* Mark Twain, Artemus Ward, Edith Wharton, Sinclair Lewis, and Theodore Dreiser were other American authors whom he admired, and, among poets, Edna St. Vincent Millay.

His one outstanding admiration among contemporary English novelists was Thomas Hardy. On an occasion of their meeting at the high-table of a Cambridge college, Alfred qualified someone's statement that Hardy was his favourite novelist by saying, 'Yes, next to Jane Austen', to which Hardy replied, 'Well, of course, it's the greater thing'. 'What he meant by that', said Alfred, 'I'm sure I don't know.'

Probably he on y meant to be modest; for though Jane Austen did her job to perfection, she wrote only of small things in a small world: characters as nobly conceived as those of Hardy at his best were altogether beyond her range.

Subsequently Alfred spent a week-end with Hardy at Dorchester, his fellow-guests, whom he then met for the first time, being Edward Clodd and Arthur Symons.

When they retired to their rooms for the night they found that Hardy had considerately placed by the bed-side of each a selection of the others' works, so that by the next day they might have common ground of a literary kind for their better mutual acquaintance.

Hardy had by that time ceased from writing novels. Arthur Symons, to lure him back from verse-writing, begged that they might have 'another *Jude the Obscure*'. 'No,' said Alfred decisively, '*not* another Jude, please!' About that book, by the man he so much admired, he was apparently in agreement with Mrs. Hardy.

Another of Alfred's high admirations was Christina Rossetti, of whom he said that posterity would probably place her above Swinburne. It was an admiration which we shared; twice I had the pleasure of introducing him to poems by her which he did not know; of one he asked me to send him a copy; of the other (a poem called 'The River of Life') he said, 'Yes: it's the sort of nonsense that is worth writing', a remark which some-what consoled me for his having described certain de-votional poems of my own as 'nonsense'. Some years later he said he thought they were the 'cleverest' I had ever written; from which I gathered that with him 'nonsense' as applied to poetry was not a word of opprobrium.

This was borne out later when in *The Name and Nature of Poetry* he expressed his high admiration for certain poems which, in his view, had no discoverable meaning, and might therefore be classed as nonsense, yet without losing their claim to be regarded also as good poetry.

His memory of poetry was extraordinary, even of poetry for which he had no special admiration. One day we were discussing Keble, a poet for whom by nature he had not much liking, though in *The Name and Nature of Poetry* he had taken the trouble to say which of all his poems he considered to be the best. I happened to have mentioned the hymn which begins 'Sun of my soul, thou Saviour dear', saying that it only formed part of a whole poem, the first verse of which I was unable to remember. Immediately he quoted it with unhesitating correctness. Possibly it was early reading, or perhaps learning by heart things which his mother chose for him, that gave that verse from Keble its long hold on his memory. Yet I could give other instances not limited to

He did not care much for Landor's prose writing: he had even said that Landor's were the emptiest books that ever pretended to be full; yet when I sent him a quotation I could not trace to its right author he placed it for me at once in one of the *Imaginary Conversations*.

NOTES AND CRITICISMS

As a rule A.E.H. kept what he called his 'pedantry' separate from his poetry, but in the one of his note-books which contained entries designed for the slaying of false reputations I found the following lines, a sort of send-off to the barbed criticisms which came after. Who 'Nicolas and Karl' were I do not know; classical scholars can probably identify them.

> Gross weighs the mounded marl
> On Nicolas and Karl;
> Dance on their graves, and they will never rage.
> Now 'tis the turn of men that cannot think,
> And yet delight to wet the pen in ink
> And watch the goose-quill, all the worse for drink,
> Pursue ancestral instinct on the page.
> They, they must lift their voice,
> And teach their grandmothers, and prattle rules:
> This neither is their courage nor their choice,
> But their necessity in being fools.

This was followed by about five pages of the stored ammunition which I have already mentioned. A few of the commentaries which were entered in the note-book had names attached to them; but others (those designed for dunces and fools) seemed merely to be awaiting personal application as occasion might serve.

Of Professor Robinson Ellis (whose mind he kindly classed as that of an idiot child) he wrote: 'Mr. Ellis' reluctance to accept the emendations of others is only equalled by the reluctance of others to accept the emendations of Mr. Ellis.'

Of Professor Jebb: 'Jebb is the Lewis Morris of scholarship.'

Of Mrs. Meynell: 'She has a temperament which she mistakes for an intellect.'

Of Swinburne (for whose poetry he had a genuine admiration – up to a certain date) he wrote, of what came subsequently: 'Mr. Swinburne no longer writes poetry: he only makes a clattering noise'; and added: 'Swinburne has now said not only all he has to say about everything, but all he has to say about nothing.'

But his treatment of these, though it erred on the side of severity, was mild by comparison with what he meted out to those objects of his special aversion, the pretentious fools who with misled minds strayed mischievously into his own special department of textual criticism. Of the jolly ferocity with which he was prepared to put these into their places, I give here a few samples which had no names attached to them, in order that any who are not readers of the edited classics or the learned reviews, may get an idea of that gift for invective which made him the most feared, and perhaps also the most hated, among the pedants (his own pet phrase) of his day.

'When ―― has acquired a scrap of misinformation he cannot rest till he has imparted it.'

'Nature, not content with denying to Mr. ―― the faculty of thought, has endowed him with the faculty of writing.'

'I do not know upon what subject ―― w'll next employ his versatile incapacity. He is very well – dangerously well.'

'If we all knew as little as ―― does, we should doubtless find the classics as easy as he does.'

'Conjectural emendation as practised by ―― is not a

game, an exercise requiring skill and heed, like marbles or skittles or cats'-cradle, but a pastime, like leaning against a wall and spitting.'

'—— usually has the last word in controversy because he incurs exposures which editors do not like to print.'

'I can easily understand why Mr. —— should not tell the truth about other people. He fears reprisals: he apprehends that they may tell the truth about *him*.'

'If Mr. —— were a postage-stamp he would be a very good postage-stamp; but adhesiveness is not the virtue of a critic. A critic is free and detached.'

Sometimes, of course, as is inevitable with one who has this illustrative gift, his statements were imaginative rather than literal. When he wrote: 'I could train a dog to edit the classics like Mr. ——', it was not true, but it conveyed truth. Less extreme, but equally untrue, was his declaration to someone who was sentimentalizing over the song of the skylark: 'If you will equip me with a balloon, a kettle, and a bunch of keys, I will undertake to make a better noise than any song-lark.' But who can grudge him an untruthfulness so suggestively conveyed? And when he wrote: 'The rules of criticism are nothing to me nor to any critic: they exist for the guidance of learners, the support of imbeciles, and the restraint of maniacs',[1] he put in an exaggerated form something that is well worth pondering. Of an argument that had no sense in it

[1] A revised version, in the 1911 Inaugural Lecture, ran: Rules of criticism were framed by the benevolent for the guidance, the support and the restraint of three classes of persons: they are leading-strings for infants, they are crutches for cripples, and they are strait-waistcoats for maniacs.

he wrote: 'I shall never understand it – not if I live till I die.'

What all this goes mainly to show is that while Alfred considered the exposure of false pretensions to be his duty as a critic and a scholar, he enjoyed telling the truth provocatively. And he did this not only when dealing with persons but with things in general and with morals in particular, illustrative of which was his remark (I believe that Anatole France made a similar pronouncement) that the rarest of sexual aberrations is chastity. It is quite true, but it could hardly be said in a more provocative way.

Equally aggressive was his statement that morality, like religion, is chiefly prized by men as an excuse for making others unhappy.

It was often the same in social matters. When an unfortunate friend of mine, meeting him for the first time in Cambridge, ventured on self-introduction by saying, 'I have the pleasure of knowing your brother Laurence,' Alfred replied stiffly, 'Knowing my brother Laurence is no introduction to *me*.' After which my friend was greatly surprised to find that we were on speaking terms; and I had to explain that all Alfred meant, in that very pointed rebuff, was that he did not want to have the trouble of talking to him.

But in spite of his silence and exclusiveness he had a gift for winning the regard of others, perhaps more fully than he returned it. When he left the Patent Office to become Professor of Latin at University College, London, he received from a colleague a letter which pays so warm a tribute to his character, especially in relation to friends, that I cannot refrain from quoting it:

Dear Housman,

I got your testimonials this morning, and shortly afterwards I found that your name was in the *Times* as Professor of Latin to London University. I am as delighted with your success as though I had got something for myself. Now mind, that's saying as much as one can say about anyone else's good fortune. W———'s remark that your success was a score for the Office excited my anger. I told him that it was a score for you, and that it was nothing at all for the infernal Office. It is funny to think how I used to chaff you about your work producing no money, and all the time you were working silently on, with that strength of purpose which I can admire but can't imitate . . . As a rule English people never allow themselves to say or write what they think about anyone, no matter how much of a pal he may be. Well, I am going to let myself loose. I like you better than any man I ever knew. There is, as far as I could ever discover, absolutely no flaw in your character as a man, and no one would ever hope for a better friend. I don't say this only on my own account, but I have seen how you can stick to a friend like you have to Jackson. I mean stick to him in the sentimental sense of not forgetting him although he is right out of your reach. I have always, besides liking you so much, had a great respect for your

learning. I always do respect a man who can do anything well. Now your work has produced for you
substantial honour, I feel proud of your success, and I
hope that you will be much happier altogether. I know
you must naturally feel proud. If you don't, you are a
duffer. One doesn't get too many moments of elation
in this life, so don't check the feeling when you have it.
The testimonials are wonderfully good. At one o'clock
or thereabouts, Kingsford and I will drink a glass of the
old Falernian to your long life and increasing prosperity.
Dear old pal, I'm as pleased as if I'd done something
good myself.

Yours faithfully, . . .

This is quoted without the permission of the writer,
for it is without address and I cannot read the signature.
But if that correspondent of forty-six years back is still
living, it may please him to know that his letter was kept
undestroyed among my brother's papers, and that I
found it lying alongside another letter – the last which
he ever received from the greatest of all his friends,
the Jackson above referred to.

But Alfred did not keep only the letters of his friends;
sometimes letters from strangers who pestered him have
survived – mainly, perhaps, because on the back sheet
is pencilled a rough draft of his reply. Here is one to
someone who, having been refused permission to quote
one of his poems, wrote to complain in an injured
tone:

Sir,

Permission to quote is one thing: permission to misquote is another. First you take certain verses of mine and disfigure them with illiterate alterations, then you ask me to let you attribute them publicly to me; and now, because I do not abet you in injuring my reputation, you think it 'rather hard'.

Oh, why was Burton built on Trent!

That last sentence is explained by the fact that Burton-on-Trent was the address of his correspondent.

Alfred's minute insistence on accuracy is well exemplified in his reply to a friend who regretted that she had been unable to obtain a first edition of *Last Poems* and had been obliged to content herself with the second. 'In that case', he wrote, 'you have the more valuable edition. In the first two commas are missing.'

WITH FRIENDS AND ACQUAINTANCES

Since my brother's death there has been a persistent attempt, because of his reserve and reticence, to make him out a man of mystery. It is quite true that he kept himself rigidly aloof from all but a small circle of friends, and having no 'small talk' of his own, mixed ill in the company of people who did not interest him. But with those he knew better he liked well to sit and be talked to, so long as they did not expect him to say much in return; and those who were not easy talkers themselves found this an effort.

Even in the most intellectual company he preferred to remain silent; Robert Bridges, to whom he paid a short visit, could get no talk out of him, yet afterwards Alfred wrote telling me how very well they had agreed on certain important literary and political matters. Wilfrid Scawen Blunt wrote of him in his reminiscences: 'He would, I think, be quite silent if he were allowed to be.' 'That', said Alfred, when I told him of it, 'is absolutely true.' And often when I and other members of the family were with him, we had to do all the talking, working hard to keep him interested, and not always quite sure that we were succeeding.

But there was nothing mysterious about it; it was merely temperamental disinclination to talk for the sake of talking, combined with a proud shyness lest he should give himself away cheaply to those who would not value a gift that came with effort.

Socially this proud shyness made him difficult to get on with – not always, however. Among his friends he was differently reported of – some found him impenetrably silent, others genially conversational – and it was not a question of liking or not liking. The reason, I think, was simple: those whom his shyness embarrassed kept him shy; with those whom it did not embarrass his shyness went. Even in his own family this difference was to be noted. Clemence and I were the embarrassed ones:

Kate, who was probably his favourite, rather less so; Basil and his wife not at all. And, as a consequence, from the last named comes a testimonial to his easy sociability and his power to charm and amuse when he was in the mood for it, which for others, even of his closest acquaintances, was non-existent. This is from a letter written by this sister-in-law after my brother's death:

'There is one thing I don't understand in all that is written about Alfred – they all speak as if he never had any happiness in life; surely that cannot be true. I never knew that side of his life, he always seemed to enjoy things and to be happy, and enjoy amusing others with his clever nonsense. I have known him and Basil laugh until they cried. It hurts to think of him not getting some real happiness out of life, he deserved it, apart from his success and fame that must have given him satisfaction; but his kindness to others must have meant pleasure to him also.'

Jokes he did certainly enjoy when they seemed good to him, and he liked telling them. Usually when he did so his manner was dry and precise – quite effective in its way; but occasionally something would strike him as so ludicrous that it simply bowled him over, and laughter became the accompaniment. One of his friends tells of a joke which so tickled him that he could hardly get it out. Yet the joke was a very simple one; and if I told it here, readers might not see in it much to laugh at.

But though he had a cheerful side which showed only to a few, there was the other by which he was more generally known. An article in the *New Statesman* (May 9th, 1936) by his friend Mr. Percy Withers, whom he often visited (which he would not have done had it not given him satisfaction), gives the more sombre view of him; and while there is nothing in it which one can question there is also nothing to cast doubt on his real friendship toward the writer:

'The depths and complexities of Housman's character were almost impenetrably obscured by his reticence, and still more perhaps by his determined habit of self-suppression. In the early days of friendship I could only attribute his unyielding patches of taciturnity to my own insufficiencies, and so probably made confusion worse confounded. Until one day, immediately following his visit to Mr. and Mrs. Bridges, Robert Bridges vociferated in a breath: "Can you get him to talk? I can't." This was appeasing, and still more so when a universally popular Head of College regaled me with the inconspicuous devices he had resorted to in the capacity of host to limit their unsupported interviews to ten minutes at a stretch. True, Housman could never be garrulous, the easy and traditional exchanges of personalities seemed impossible to him; and except good stories were passing, never jocund. But search his knowledge, suggest and question with discrimination, refuse defeat, and the reward was converse not brilliant, but rich in information, excellently clear and incisive in expression, prompt in

G
97

analogy and quotation, whether in prose or verse, and, perhaps its rarest quality, judgments and opinions that were never perverse or whimsical, but the fruits of a mind trained to precision, amazingly retentive, and exquisitively sensitive to literary values. His assessments of literary merit were always given with decision, in the case of poetry with an air of finality; almost they brought conviction when least anticipated. . . . What was and what was not poetry he decided simply, and I should say with the nearest possible approach to infallibility, by the physical response, or none, in the throat, the spinal cord, or the pit of the stomach, and the last the supreme oracle. Once when he had used the term in conversation, he was asked, What is the solar plexus? A doctor present was hastening the Faculty's definition, when Housman whipped in with the rejoinder "It is what my poetry comes from . . . " The emotions may have run as deep and strong in many men, but few can have repressed them so effectually that only intimacy provided a rare and fleeting glimpse. The consequence was, for him, loneliness; for most of those who knew him a half-knowledge — the half that tended to exclude those feelings that are the better part of friendship. He seemed neither to ask nor expect affection, but when, on the two or three occasions he either related or received in my presence unquestionable evidences of it, he described the effect as almost overwhelming. A common enough phrase, but coming from such a man as Housman a revelation of qualities hidden too deep away, and of potentialities, I cannot but think, grievously and mistakenly thwarted.'

In a private letter, written subsequently, Mr. Withers, giving an account of A.E.H.'s last visit, says: 'I know he was happy with us. He came so willingly, even fixed his visits two or three months in advance, and always seemed so thoroughly at home. He liked my wife, he recognized her efficiency in the whole province of huswifery and her quietude – she never bothered him.'

That sentence contains what, for him, were all the commendatory virtues: it was only with women who never bothered him that he could make friends.

What Alfred thought about himself in his personal relations has been written for him by another. In *Seven Pillars of Wisdom* T. E. Lawrence gives the following introspective account of himself:

'There was my craving to be liked – so strong and nervous that never could I open myself friendly to another. The terror of failure in an effort so important made me shrink from trying; besides, there was the standard; for intimacy seemed shameful unless the other could make the perfect reply, in the same language, after the same method, for the same reasons.

'There was a craving to be famous; and a horror of being known to like being known. Contempt for my passion for distinction made me refuse every offered honour. . . .'

Against this passage, Alfred wrote in the margin, 'This is me'.

COLLEGE LIFE AND CAMBRIDGE

While there is no doubt that his Professorship at University College, London, released Alfred from the dull bondage of work that was wasteful of his time and abilities, it did not give him the full scope that he required for the application of his classical learning in the teaching of others. That only came nineteen years later, when in 1911 he was appointed Kennedy Professor of Latin at Cambridge, and, at the same time, was made a Fellow of Trinity. From then on, he was in his right setting, and if one may judge by appearances, and by an amiability in social intercourse which became more apparent as years went on, was thenceforward happier both in mind and circumstance than at any previous period since his break with Oxford.

But if, as he declared, Oxford had influenced him little, it is curious that he should have remained so much an Oxford man in sentiment, always wishing that Oxford should win the Boat Race, and addressing men who had like himself come from Oxford to Cambridge as 'fellow-exiles'.

It was when speaking at some such gathering that he made the remark: 'After having been at Cambridge for twenty years, I realize that it is an asylum in all senses of the word.' And when taken to task by a Trinity Fellow for having said it, he replied: 'Well, I suppose I did say something of the sort: but it was to an Oxford audience.'

At the farewell dinner given to him by University College, London, on his appointment as Kennedy Professor of Latin, he said something about himself which was even more joyously improper. After referring to the deplorable abstemiousness of Professor Mayor, and the strain which the duty of restoring good living would put upon his successor, he added: 'So the University which once saw Wordsworth drunk and once saw Porson sober will see a better scholar than Wordsworth, and a better poet than Porson, betwixt and between.'

At another valedictory gathering on that occasion, when his students presented him with a large silver loving-cup, he told them that he was succeeding a man at Cambridge 'who drank like a fish – if drinking nothing but water could be so described'.

This loving-cup had round it an inscription in capitals, a little hard to read: and when he first showed it to me, I said 'Is this Latin?' 'No,' he replied, 'English, very good English.' The words were: MALT DOES MORE THAN MILTON CAN TO JUSTIFY GOD'S WAYS TO MAN.

Though Alfred cared little for the criticism of the papers, he liked to know what they said of him, and paid regularly for press-cuttings. One day in February 1911 he sent me the following extract from the *St. James's Gazette*:

'I was a little surprised to see that Professor A. E. Housman, who is now worthily seated in the chair of the late Professor Mayor at Cambridge, receives in the new *Encyclopaedia Britannica* only a few lines at the end of an article on his brother, Mr. Laurence Housman. This is, I think, to measure more by bulk than by weight.'

Underlining the last sentence, he wrote against it 'Ha, ha! I did not write this, but I paid for it.'

It was a case of log-rolling; I had a friend in the editorial department of the *Encyclopaedia Britannica* who had done me that one-sided kindness. The omission, I believe, has since been handsomely repaired: but even the Chambers' *Cyclopaedia of English Literature*, which should have known better, in the edition of 1903 had given us similar wrong measure.

People seem to have got the impression that Alfred disliked being questioned about his poems. That was not my own experience; if the question had any interest in it he liked answering it. I asked him once whether, as a rule, his so happily-chosen adjectives had come to him spontaneously or after labour and with difficulty; and I gave as an instance 'coloured counties', a phrase which has become famous. 'Now, that you should have picked that out', he said, 'is interesting. When I wrote the poem I put down, just to fill up for the time, a quite ordinary adjective, which didn't satisfy me; others followed. Then with the poem in my head, I went to bed and dreamed, and in my dream I hit on the word "painted"; when I woke up I saw that "painted" wouldn't do, but it gave me "coloured" as the right word.'

This is confirmed in the first draft of the poem which

I found in one of his note-books, where the alternatives run: sunny, pleasant, checkered, patterned; 'painted' is left out, it was not necessary for that to be written down – it had suggested the right word.

That was the only occasion on which a dream gave him real help in the composition of a poem; but he did, on at least two other occasions, dream verses of a sort, which he was able to remember and write down on waking. One of these – a poem (the author of which, in his dream, was not himself, but G. K. Chesterton) ran as follows:

> When I was born in a world of sin,
> Praise be God it was raining gin;
> Gin on the house, gin on the walls,
> Gin on the bun-shops and copy-book stalls.

The other poem is not of sufficient meaning or substance to be worth quoting. More important help came to him once from a paragraph in a daily paper. On August 6th, 1895, a young Woolwich Cadet, aged eighteen, took his own life, leaving a long letter addressed to the Coroner to say why he had done so. The gist of that letter was quoted in a newspaper-cutting of the day, which I found lying in my brother's copy of *A Shropshire Lad* alongside the poem which begins:

> Shot? so quick, so clean an ending?

It is quite evident that certain passages in that letter

prompted the writing of the poem; one sentence indeed is almost quoted. I give here only that part of the letter which bears most closely on the poem:

'I wish it to be clearly understood that I am not what is commonly called "temporarily insane", and that I am putting an end to my life after several weeks of careful deliberation. I do not think that I need justify my actions to anyone but my Maker, but . . . I will state the main reasons which have determined me. The first is utter cowardice and despair. There is only one thing in this world which would make me thoroughly happy; that one thing I have no earthly hope of obtaining. The second – which I wish was the only one – is that I have absolutely ruined my own life; but I thank God that as yet, so far as I know, I have not morally injured, or "offended", as it is called in the Bible, anyone else. Now I am quite certain that I could not live another five years without doing so, and for that reason alone, even if the first did not exist, I should do what I am doing. . . . At all events it is final, and consequently better than a long series of sorrows and disgraces.'

How close to that come the lines:

> 'Oh soon, and better so than later
> After long disgrace and scorn,
> You shot dead the household traitor,
> The soul that should not have been born.'

The jury brought in the usual verdict. I give no name; but should the date serve as a guide, there may yet be some living whom it will gratify to know that a young life wrecked forty-two years ago left inspiration for another that was worth the having.

I have given in earlier pages instances of Alfred's ruthless treatment of intellectual foolishness, more especially of foolishness which gave itself the airs of learning. In that direction he could be cruel with relish: but toward moral foolishness, especially toward the foolishness of troubled youth, his inclination was all the other way. Even deflections from rectitude which he would not have tolerated in himself, caused no withdrawal of aid when once it had been proffered; and in a case known to me, conduct which he described as 'nefarious' did not alter relations of real personal friendship between him and the offender, though the offence was to himself.

Certain 'laws of God and man', with their socially imposed sanctions, he disliked heartily, and with recognition of human nature's imperfect material, made a wide allowance for its failures. This is shown clearly in many of his published poems; and especially among those from which a final selection has now been made, in the one which I have placed last (p. 226), which, though somewhat lacking in literary quality, is so strong an expression of his feeling against social injustice that I am sure he would have wished it to be known.

Among his papers which I had to go through after his death, I found frequent evidence of his generosity, both moral and monetary (lenient in the one case, lavish in the other) toward people whose claim on him was small, but whose importunity was great. His kindness of tone (he kept copies of his replies) to those he had once befriended never varied, even when he had to reject further applications for aid – applications which, in one case, persisted with brazen effrontery even after his death. He was equally and spontaneously generous toward the National Exchequer in its time of need. At the beginning of the War he sent the Chancellor a donation of several hundred pounds, and again during the financial crisis in 1931, when the National Government was first formed, came to the rescue so far as his means allowed.

On various occasions he did the same for members of his own family; and about the time of his return from Oxford, when his own need was probably greatest, he surrendered for the payment of certain debts his entire share of a bequest which had just come to us from the death of a relative.

He had apparently, unknown to his family, consider-able ability for the ordering and keeping of accounts; and at University College, while serving on a sub-com-mittee of Finance, he drew up reports which make good reading. In one of them he sets out to describe the vary-ing degrees of reluctance shown by Professors and Fellows to pay their dues; and on reading it I was reminded of a story he once told me of an amateur tithe-collector who undertook to secure for his rector the payments which were overdue, and wrote to his debtors, 'If you do not send me a cheque by return I shall do something which will greatly astonish you.' In a more sedate form A.E.H.'s manipulation of the backward ones was somewhat similar.

On other occasions he was required to write for his College, or for the University, certain official addresses and letters of ceremony; and this he did in correct style with the utmost decorum. The Address from the University of Cambridge to the King upon the occasion of his Jubilee, which was A.E.H.'s composition, is here given as an example of his literary style in the service of officialdom, excellent of its kind, but not, I should imagine, a job which he much enjoyed. Indeed, I remember his saying that it had given, him a lot of trouble:

To the King's most excellent Majesty.

We, the Chancellor, Masters, and Scholars of the University of Cambridge, desire to approach You with our loyal and dutiful congratulations on the completion of the twenty-fifth year of Your Majesty's reign.

The events of that reign, for greatness and moment, are such as have rarely been comprised within twenty-five years of human history. It has witnessed unexampled acceleration in the progress of man's acquaintance with the physical universe, his mastery of the forces of nature, and his skill in their application to the processes of industry and to the arts of life. No less to the contrivance of havoc and destruction has the advance of knowledge imparted new and prodigious efficacy; and it has been the lot of Your Majesty to confront at the head of your people the most formidable assault which has ever been delivered upon the safety and freedom of these realms. By exertion and sacrifice that danger was victoriously repelled; and Your Majesty's subjects, who have looked abroad upon the fall of states, the dissolution of systems, and a continent parcelled out anew, enjoy beneath your sceptre the retrospect of a period acquainted indeed with anxieties even within the body politic and perplexed by the emergence of new and difficult problems, but harmoniously combining stability with progress and rich in its contribution of benefits to the health and welfare of the community. . . .

Called suddenly to the throne in an hour of vehement political contention, Your Majesty gave early evidence of the qualities which have since proved equal to every occasion. Courage and composure, steadfast impartiality, wise judgment and delicate feeling have ever been present and manifest; and a transparent openness of nature has knit Your Majesty to the affections of all your subjects, who, without respect of rank or condition, are conscious of what we may presume to call a fellow-feeling with their sovereign. That Your Majesty, with your august and beloved Consort at your side, may be granted long life and happy continuance of the blessings vouch-safed to your reign in the years already numbered is the earnest prayer of this University, even as it is the common hope of a people fortunate in their King and grateful for their fortune.

His willingness to undertake a task which, though distasteful, he probably knew that he could do well, is an example of his kindly acquiescence to the desires of others in matters which gave him a lot of trouble; how much trouble is vividly illustrated in the following letter, declining the post of Public Orator to the University of Cambridge which had been offered him.

Trinity College
3 Jan. 1920.

My dear Parry,[1]

I must begin with grateful acknowledgment to you and my other friends, because I could not read your letter without feelings which had some pure pleasure in them; but this was swallowed up in surprise, and surprise itself was engulfed in horror.

Not if the stipend were £150,000 instead of £150 would I be Public Orator. I could not discharge the duties of the office without abandoning all other duties and bidding farewell to such peace of mind as I possess. You none of you have any notion what a slow and barren mind I have, nor what a trouble composition is to me (in prose, I mean: poetry is either easy or impossible). When the job is done, it may have a certain amount of form and finish and perhaps a fake air of ease; but there is an awful history behind it. The letter to Jackson[2] last year laid waste three whole mornings: the first, I sat staring in front of me and wishing for death; the second, I wrote

---

[1] R. St. J. Parry, D.D.
[2] Henry Jackson, O.M., Regius Professor of Greek.

down disjointed phrases and sentences which looked loath-
some; the third, after a night in which I suppose my
subliminal self had been busy, I had some relief in fitting
them together and finding they could be improved into
something respectable. I can stand this once in a way; but
to be doing it often, and have it always hanging over one,
and in connexion with subjects much less congenial than
Jackson, I could not bear.

The University has been very good to me, and has
given me a post in which I have duties which are not disagreeable, and opportunity for studies which I enjoy and
in which I can hope to do the University credit; and I
should not really be doing it a good turn if I sacrificed that
work, as I must, to the performance, even if more efficient
than mine would be, of the duties of the Orator.

Do not think this an unkind reply to a kind letter. I
have also written to Jackson, as an interview would be
useless, and distressing to both of us.

Yours sincerely
A. E. Housman.

In politics he stayed aloof, over the benefit of
democratic government being a complete sceptic. He
even believed that slavery was essential to a well-
governed State, but was so English in his preferences
that he probably considered England a better-governed
country under democratic mismanagement than any
other favoured with a form of despotism of which,
theoretically, he more greatly approved.

He conformed similarly in the outward observances
of religion, approving of the Church of England as an
institution, while having no faith in its tenets. This
conformity even extended to his receiving the Com-
munion when staying with his stepmother or friends who
were church-people; and this though, as he told me, it had
meant nothing to him even when he was confirmed.
Probably he did this because it helped him to feel nearer
to those he cared for, and while doing him no harm gave
them pleasure.

It may have been that same attitude of mind which
made him, in his last illness, find physical relief through
the influence of other people's religious goodwill. He
told the sister in charge of him as he lay ill, of his knowledge of another sister who prayed for him nightly, and
he said he liked it and it did him good. He asked the
nursing sister to pray too; and would tell her in the
morning that the prayers had 'worked'.

HONOURS DECLINED

During the years following his appointment to the
Kennedy Chair of Latin at Cambridge, A.E.H. had
received offers of Academic honours from various
Universities, and had declined all of them. Glasgow
University indeed had offered him the Honorary Degree
of Doctor of Laws as early as 1905; St. Andrews did the

same in 1922. Then followed offers of Honorary Degrees of various kinds from Cambridge in 1928, Liverpool in 1931, and North Wales in 1934. The proposal from his own University of Oxford to confer on him the honorary degree of Doctor of Letters he twice refused, in 1928 and 1934.

In all his replies, after due thanks, he excused himself from explaining the reason for his refusal. But in declining to be nominated for election as a Fellow of the British Academy in 1911 he described the honour as one which he 'should not find congenial nor feel to be appropriate'.

It was about six years ago that he admitted to me another refusal which, till then, he had kept secret. I had for some time felt a brotherly concern that the one honour which I thought he would be willing to accept, the Order of Merit, had not been offered him. Since others were feeling as I did, I broached the question – would he accept it? He replied that he would not, and when, disappointed, I asked why, he said that, though he had always known that it would be offered him if he lived to the age of eighty, he had decided against accepting any honour, and against this particular one because it was not always given to the right persons. He had condoled, he said, with Robert Bridges for having had to receive the honour at the same time as John Galsworthy, whose writing they both disliked, and Bridges had admitted that the circumstance had not given him pleasure.

I suppose I pressed him further, for suddenly he blushed (an unexpected gift which he had retained from the days of his youth) and said: 'Well, as a matter of fact, Mr. Baldwin did write to me not long ago to say that the King was ready to offer it; and I believe it was offered at the same time to Bernard Shaw. But for the reason I have already stated, and because I could not have the trouble of going to be received by the King, I declined. But,' he added, 'I don't want it to be known; it wouldn't be fair to the King.'

Who first gave away the secret I do not know. It was only after my brother's death that I found that others knew of it, and that word of it had gone to the Press.

His letter to the King's secretary, declining the honour, was as follows:

'With all gratitude for His Majesty's most kind and flattering wish to confer upon me the Order of Merit, I humbly beg permission to decline this high honour. I hope to escape the reproach of thanklessness or churlish behaviour by borrowing the words in which an equally loyal subject, Admiral Cornwallis, declined a similar mark of the Royal favour: "I am, unhappily, of a turn of mind that would make my receiving that honour the most unpleasant thing imaginable." '

In the official reply, he was assured that His Majesty would appreciate his reasons for this decision, which, considering the final phrase of the quotation defining them, indicated a remarkable power of sympathy on the part of His Majesty.

When Alfred and I were together on holiday two years before his death, he became more open in his talk, both about our past family history and other matters personal to himself, than he had ever been previously; it seemed that he wished me to know certain things which I had not known before. It was then that he talked about our mother for the first time that I can remember. Maintaining his reserve over certain related matters, he said, without my having asked, 'More I shall not tell you.'

We talked a good deal about his poems, as I was anxious to make sure of what I might or might not do over any future publication. 'New Year's Eve', the poem which he published in a magazine while at Oxford, he ruled out; it smacked too much of the Swinburnian style which he had abandoned. He wrote it, he said, in his twentieth year. 'I was then a deist.' 'And now', I asked, 'what do you call yourself – an agnostic?' 'No,' he said decisively. 'I am an atheist.' He then went on to say that he thought the Church of England the best religion ever invented; it was less disturbing than other forms, and eliminated 'so much Christian nonsense'. Christianity, he added, was most harmful in its social application. This was said in answer to a remark of mine that a great many people, while rejecting theological Christianity, had now come to accept Christ's ethical teaching as the only sane and safe way of life in this world, whether there were a future life or no.

Belief in immortality was quite unnecessary, he said, for good morals. The Hebrews had a higher code of morals than the Egyptians, and did not allow themselves to be perverted from non-belief in a future life by Egyptian superstition. The Sadducees represented the orthodox religion of their race: the Pharisees were the modernists. He mentioned the difficulty some missionaries had with a South African tribe who had no religion at all, and therefore no word for God. So they searched for the thing the natives most valued and desired, and finding it to be 'decomposing meat', gave that name to God. I have myself heard a similar story of the trouble missionaries have had to find the word for love, 'appetite for food' being the nearest equivalent.

Referring to the story which had been published in the Bromsgrove School Magazine, he said that the best part had been cut out. The people in it worshipped a god called Goodness Gracious, who originally demanded the sacrifice of young children. Then when babies ran short, someone had the idea of substituting kid-dolls which made a screaming noise in the fire; and finding that these satisfied him equally well, they experimented in a cheaper kind; and finally (as nothing made any difference) they sacrificed whatever they could spare best and would miss least. At the date when the story opened they were piously sacrificing a diseased potato-crop, which the god seemed to like as well as anything.

He said that when at Oxford he found he could imitate Swinburne quite as well as – sometimes, he thought, better than – the original, but even then he thought the Swinburnian method wrong.

He had been friendly with Robert Bridges. 'An amazing man', he said; 'gets up at five and makes his own coffee, though well up in the eighties.' But he was in more agreement with him over politics than over poetry. With reference to his too-free theory of scansion Alfred had once challenged him as to how a certain line should be read, stating his own objection to both ways. Bridges said, 'Does it matter?' Neither way seemed to offend his less sensitive ear.

When I told him how, on meeting Professor Robinson Ellis in 1901, I found him quite unaware of Alfred's having written any poems, 'Then', said Alfred, 'you educated him; for, when Quiller-Couch published his *Oxford Book of English Verse*, Ellis wrote to reproach him for not including something from *A Shropshire Lad*.'

Of the reputation which his poems won for him he wrote recently to an American correspondent: 'Though it gives me no lively pleasure, it is something like a mattress interposed between me and the hard ground.'

Those words were written when life was ceasing to have any comfort for him, and had, I should imagine, only a late application; for I am sure the success of his poems had given him satisfaction.

LAST YEARS

Of Alfred's life during his later years, I think it may be said that fundamentally it was sombre and sometimes sad, but incidentally not lacking either in interest or amusement. He became more communicative, and showed a more ready interest than formerly in the concerns of others; and in this self-release from long-accustomed reserve he adopted the kindly practice of sending about once a year a selection of his nonsense rhymes to certain members of his family, more especially to his invalid brother, Basil, who received them with delight and passed copies on to the rest of us. Some of the verses are here included; probably the whole lot were sent to him at one time or another. I gather from their place in the note-books that their composition extended over a good many years. Most of them were written off-hand; but several of them had been as much corrected as his more serious poems.

Though Alfred's health caused him both discomfort and depression during his last years, he was sometimes able to joke about it; and even on the fair copy which I possess of the poem written for his own funeral one finds appended two jocular comments. In the second line of the first verse he had originally written 'Through time and space to roam'; in the rough draft he altered 'space' into 'place', and then, on the fair copy, entered a gibing note about the printers' probable insistence on 'space' as the right word. Finally, below the last verse, he wrote: 'And then, unless forcibly restrained, the choir will sing –' then followed the conventional 'Gloria' – an ascription of praise unsuitable for the very impersonal Power to whom the poem was addressed.

In the last year or so, the stairs to his rooms gave him increasing trouble. One night, returning with a friend from a convivial gathering, and exchanging by the way stories more diverting than decorous, he stopped to say as they parted, 'I hope you will remember, if I am found dead at the top of my stairs to-morrow, that our last conversation was edifying.'

Of what remains to be recorded, I cannot do better than give once again what has already appeared in my book of reminiscences, *The Unexpected Years*.

About three years before the end, his health began rapidly to decline, and his walking power, which all his life had given that quiet companionship of nature which suited him best, had considerably diminished. For some years he had been taking holidays abroad, generally in France. In 1935, after a slight accident, he had almost decided not to go abroad again; and it was then that he wrote telling me he had begun to obey his doctor's orders to the extent of only walking twice as far as what was medically permitted him. At that time his rooms in Trinity College were on the second floor, forty steps up. 'I still go up my 44 stairs', he wrote, 'two at a time, but that is in hopes of dropping dead at the top.' It was the expression (merely verbal then, I think) of a wish which from that time on became more definite, not to outlive his physical enjoyment of life.

Fortunately during his last two years I was able to arrange that we should take holidays together; and in the summer of 1934, staying at Droitwich, only six miles

from our old home, we made long motor-rounds daily
through Worcestershire, Gloucestershire, Herefordshire,
and Shropshire. But in 1935, owing to his declining
health and disinclination for exertion, he elected, instead
of going as we had proposed into Yorkshire, to stay
in Cambridge; and with that as our centre we visited
more places, churches, abbeys and cathedrals than I
can count. He knew them nearly all and had a marvel-
lous memory for their main points of interest and their
style of architecture – even for those which he had not
seen for a score of years. There was hardly a cathedral
in England that he did not remember better than I did;
architecture was an interest which we shared deeply;
and our only difference was that I preferred Norman and
he Early English. 'Of course', he said dryly, as if to
discount the genuineness of my preference, 'to extol
Norman is now the fashion.' But he himself considered
that one of the duties of architecture, and especially of
windows, was to let in light, though writing of Milan
Cathedral a good many years before he had said that its
darkness was 'a fault on the right side'. Monastic gloom
did not now please him as much as it pleased me. It was
soon after that expedition that he went abroad – to
France for the last time, and there, meeting with a slight
accident, came back not much benefited.

In November 1935 I went to speak at a Peace Meeting
in Cambridge: he was then staying temporarily at the
Nursing Home which had by that time become his
accustomed place of refuge whenever his health failed.

I went to see him; he knew what I was there for: the evening before there had been a torchlight procession to advertise the meeting. 'Last night', he said, 'your people were making a great noise outside, disturbing everyone. If that is what you call a "Peace-movement" I would prefer that it should remain sedentary.'

Early in January 1936 his condition became so serious that he was not expected to live more than another week; but when the beginning of term approached, he announced his intention of leaving the Nursing Home and returning to his rooms to give his lectures. His doctor told him that this was impossible. But he insisted on doing it, with a sort of grim pleasure in being able to carry on in spite of physical weakness. At the end of term, writing to a member of the family, he said that he had never lectured better in his life. But the effort sent him back to the Nursing Home, from which he went, at the commencement of the Easter term, and gave two lectures, sitting down. That was the end.

After his death I went to stay in his rooms at Trinity, a new set of rooms on the ground floor, to which, without any trouble to himself, he and his belongings had been moved through the devoted service of his friend and co-Fellow, Mr. Andrew Gow. His bed-maker said to me: 'I loved your brother. When I first began to do for him, I used to be afraid to go into the room; but it was all right when I got to know him.' The assistant-matron at the Nursing Home said much the same; many others, whom he kept rigidly at arm's length, had a great affection for him, over and above their deep respect for his power of scholarship.

I asked his doctor how long before his death consciousness began to fail. Just about two days, I was told; but there were intervals when his mind was quite clear. And this, as far as I can remember it in his own words, is the doctor's account of their last meeting, the night before he died.

'You know', he said, 'how silent and reserved he always was; but this time he talked quite a lot and very affectionately. He held my hand for nearly half an hour. "You have been a good friend to me," he said; "I know you have brought me here so that I may not commit suicide, and I know that you may not help me to it more than the law allows. But I do ask you not to let me have any more unnecessary suffering than you can help." I told him that he should not suffer any more; and from that time on he did not. Then, to cheer him up just before I left, I told him a thoroughly naughty story. He was very weak, but he threw his head back on the pillow laughing heartily. "Yes, that's a good one," he said, "and to-morrow I shall be telling it again on the Golden Floor." '

I hope that no pious friend will try to force from that characteristic remark an interpretation implying belief in a future life, which it was most certainly not intended to convey.

Ten years before his death he wrote *For my Funeral*, the hymn which was sung at the farewell service held in

Trinity College Chapel before his body was taken up to
London for cremation. It expressed the belief that life
has no conscious hereafter.

In the chapel of Trinity College, Cambridge, a
memorial tablet has been placed bearing the following
inscription:

HOC TITVLO COMMEMORATVR

ALFRED EDWARD HOVSMAN

PER XXV ANNOS LINGVAE LATINAE PROFESSOR KENNEDIANVS

ET HVIVS COLLEGII SOCIVS

QVI BENTLEII INSISTENS VESTIGIIS

TEXTVM TRADITVM POETARVM LATINORVM

TANTO INGENII ACVMINE TANTIS DOCTRINAE COPIIS

EDITORVM SOCORDIAM

TAM ACRI CAVILLATIONE CASTIGAVIT

VT HORVM STVDIORVM PAENE REFORMATOR EXSTITERIT

IDEM POETA

TENVI CARMINVM FASCICVLO

SEDEM SIBI TVTAM IN HELICONE NOSTRO VINDICAVIT

OBIIT PRID. KAL. MAI

A.S. MCMXXXVI AETATIS SVAE LXXVII

Over the grave, where his ashes have been laid under
the north wall of the parish church at Ludlow, is a tablet
bearing these words:

LAST YEARS

IN MEMORY OF ALFRED EDWARD HOUSMAN,

M.A. OXON.

KENNEDY PROFESSOR OF LATIN AND FELLOW OF

TRINITY COLLEGE IN THE UNIVERSITY OF CAMBRIDGE.

AUTHOR OF 'A SHROPSHIRE LAD'

BORN 26 MARCH, 1859. DIED 30 APRIL, 1936.

GOOD NIGHT. ENSURED RELEASE,

IMPERISHABLE PEACE,

HAVE THESE FOR YOURS.

'Death, the most dreadful of evils, is really nothing to us; for while we are here, death is not, and when death is here, we are not. So death matters neither to the living nor to the dead.'

EPICURUS

LETTERS

LETTERS

A SELECTION OF LETTERS

THESE letters, addressed by A.E.H. mainly to members
of his own family, I have kept in separate groups, in
order to show better and without interruption, the slight
difference of style (though with common characteristics)
which he used in writing to different people; for while in
most of his letters there are touches put in purely for his
own amusement, there is also a consideration of what
will amuse and interest the recipient. Those written to
our stepmother from foreign parts were mainly of a
guide-book character, and in that respect unlike those
which he wrote to others. For the rest the differences are
slighter; but except for very short letters, he never wrote
in quite the same way to the different members of his
family; there was always a shade of distinction.

Naturally I find that I have in hand more letters
addressed to myself than to anyone else. They have a
characteristic shared by those written in his last years to
Mr. Houston Martin, a young American whose persistent
solicitations seem to have amused him – a sort of game
which he played on both of us, an amused tolerance to
which, for his own enjoyment and for our instruction, he
added a touch of benevolent depreciation: and because in

my case his general depreciation was quite genuine, I valued the more the rare bits of praise which he gave me, selecting sometimes quite unexpectedly things which I had not thought much of myself, but which – after he had praised them – went up decisively in my estimation, and have there remained.

This selection has not come from outside sources, as the result of an appeal, which might have brought me far more material than I could find use for. I merely give what has come to hand without my asking for it, or what was already in the safe keeping of various members of the family, its interest lying not so much in its biographical detail as in its portrayal of character.

From Letters to his Stepmother

These letters always began 'My dear Mamma', and were signed, 'Your loving son, A. E. Housman'.

82 Talbot Road
Bayswater. W.
29 March '85.

. . . I was delighted to get your long letter on the 26th:[1] it was quite the best epistle I have ever seen, with the possible exception of the second of the apostle Paul to the Corinthians. The violets also were very sweet: I don't know whether St. Paul used to enclose violets. Also please thank my father for his letter. Clemence and Laurence sent me a post card with a very lovely

[1] His birthday.

drawing on the back, representing Cherubim and Seraphim continually crying, and an inscription in Spanish or Portuguese, I think.

I saw the boat race yesterday, from the Thames boat house at Putney this time, so that I saw the start . . . Palm branches seemed to be the commonest decoration among the lower orders. The blue which they wore was a very artful shade, which could be made out to be either Oxford or Cambridge with equal plausibility, whichever might happen to win. . . .

The juvenile son of a friend of mine at the Office[1] has the loftiest ambition I ever heard tell of. When he goes to heaven, which he regards as a dead certainty, he wants to be *God*, and is keenly mortified to learn that it is not probable he will. However his aspirations are now turning into another channel: it has come to his knowledge, through the housemaid, that the devil has horns and a tail; and in comparison with these decorations the glories of heaven have lost their attractiveness.

An elaborate new Index of Trade Marks is being compiled at the Office. It goes on very remarkable principles which I do not quite understand. Under the head of 'Biblical Subjects' is included a picture of an old monk drinking out of a tankard; and the Virgin Mary and St. John the Baptist are put among 'Mythical Figures'. . . .

[1] The Patent Office.

10 June '85

You would never guess what I was doing on Tuesday week: serving on a Coroner's Jury. This comes of having one's name on the register of voters. Civil Servants I believe are exempt from serving on ordinary Juries, but not on Coroners'. Of course for once in a way it is rather amusing, and it is not likely to happen oftener than about once in four years. We sat on five bodies: one laundryman who tied a hundred-weight to his neck and tipped over into the water-butt; one butcher's man who cut his throat with a rusty knife and died a week after of erysipelas (moral: use a clean knife on these occasions); one old lady who dropped down in a fit; one baby who died of convulsions; and one young woman who died of heart disease after eating spring onions for supper. I really do not know what is the good of a Jury or of witnesses either; the Coroner does it all: his mind seemingly is lighted by wisdom from on high, so he tells the Jury what their verdict is and the witnesses what their evidence is: if they make mistakes he corrects them. The butcher's man had a brother-in-law: he looked radiantly happy: a member of his family had distinguished himself, and he was revelling in the reflected glory.

I think if there were an Inquest held on this Government of ours the verdict would have to be deliberate suicide: there does not seem to have been the least reason why they should have been beaten unless they wanted it. I should say whether they go out or not the whole affair will do a lot of damage to the Conservatives, because if they take office before the election they will have a fearful muddle to deal with, and if they do not, everyone will call them unpatriotic. . . .

There was a mild sort of scare at the Office the other day: a loud bang which collected quite a crowd. Civil Servants in these days of course live in hourly expectation of being blown up by dynamite for political reasons, and the Patent Office has the further danger of the ingenious and vindictive inventor of explosives, who might try to lay the place in ruins if his patent did not go smoothly. The room I sit in is considered the likeliest place, because it has a charming deep area outside, which looks as if it was made to drop dynamite into; so when this explosion was heard, several people came trooping into the room in hopes of finding corpses weltering in their gore. However they had to go empty away: I believe the noise was really the firing of a charge of powder in a neighbouring chimney to bring the soot down. . . .

25 June 1897
University College, London.

. . . I came back to town yesterday. The time I had at Bromsgrove was not bad, as either the morning or the afternoon of every day was sunny.

On the evening of the 22nd I started at eight in the evening for Clent, and got to the top of Walton Hill about 9.20. The sky was fairly clear, and so was the air to the

north, but hazy southwards: Malvern had been invisible
all day. (On Saturday when the rain was about I saw
as good a view from Walton Hill as I ever saw, the Sugar
Loaf and Black Mountain and Radnor Forest quite plain.)
One or two private bonfires started before the time, but
most of them waited for 10 o'clock. Five minutes or so
after the hour I easily counted 67. Some of these were
small affairs in the near neighbourhood, which soon
died down; but at half-past there were fifty-two burning
merrily on the south and west, from the Lickey on the
left to the Wrekin on the right. Northward I did not
attempt to count, as it was hard to tell the beacons from
the ordinary illuminations of the Black Country. Of the
distant fires Malvern was much the largest: the pile
was sixty feet high and could be seen with the naked eye
by daylight: through a telescope it looked like the Eiffel
tower, as it was much higher than its width and held
together with iron. But it had been so saturated with
paraffin that it burnt out in an hour. The Clent fire
was on the further hill, and not on the top but on the
south-western face. By midnight, the number of fires
had very much decreased, and only four, besides the
Clent one, were visible at two o'clock: two distant ones
somewhere by the Brown Clee, and two nearer, – one
Droitwich way, and one on Kinver Edge which burnt till
daylight brilliantly. It was a fine night, and at midnight
the sky in the north had enough light for me to see the
time by my watch. At two I heard a cuckoo, and
immediately afterwards the larks began to go up and

make a deafening noise, and some person at Kingswin-
ford, possibly wishing to stop the row, sent up a sky-
rocket. (There had been a number of rockets at
Birmingham before 10.) About this time the first tinge
that you could call blue came in the sky, which had
turned buff and green soon after one: at 3 the clouds were
red. I stayed to see the sun get above the mists and
clouds, which was just 4 o'clock, and then I went back to
bed at 5.15. There was a fair crowd round the Clent
fire, but a policeman, who told me at 3 that he had been
on duty ever since 6 a.m. the day before, said that it was
not near so large as in 1887. . . .

(*Portion of letter, undated, circa* 1897)

I shall be interested to see the Devotional Poems.[1]
Perhaps I myself may write a Hymn-book for use in the
Salvation Army:

> There is Hallelujah Hannah
>   Walking backwards down the lane,
> And I hear the loud Hosanna
>   Of regenerated Jane;
> And Lieutenant Isabella
>   In the centre of them comes,
> Dealing blows with her umbrella
>   On the trumpets and the drums.

Or again:[2]

It seems to come quite easy. . . .

[1] *Spikenard.*
[2] The poem that followed is given on page 59.

17 North Road, Highgate N.

22 Sept. 1897

... I came home yesterday after having been just a month away, at Paris, Rome, and Naples ... What strikes one in Paris is the countless number of handsome streets, any five of which would constitute a fine town in England: imagine a place as well built as Edinburgh or Bath and practically about as large as London. Notre-Dame is hardly equal to Westminster Abbey, and none of the modern churches are anything like St. Paul's, but the number of such buildings, interesting or beautiful, is much greater than in London; and London has nothing at all equivalent to the Louvre ... They make a deal more of their river than we do of ours: it is all edged with handsome quays and crossed with handsome bridges.

When I got into Italy the weather was very hot, and remained so all the while I was there. The Neapolitans themselves were amazed at it ... I went to Pompeii, which is more extensive than I thought, and to Vesuvius. ... When you get to the cone you begin to hear an angry sound such as water will sometimes make in pipes, as if the mountain were gargling, or were trying to talk but had stones in its mouth; which indeed it has ... It is much the highest hill in the neighbourhood, so you see all the country, vineyards and olive yards and woods of young trees, dotted with white or pink houses: into this green carpet the lava runs out on every side in long grey tongues, as if you had spilt an inkpot. There had

been an overflow about a month before I was there . . .
I went to the place: the surface had mostly turned grey,
but the red-hot part could be seen through cracks, and
the heat in some places was like a furnace. The guides
fasten coins to the end of long sticks, plunge them into
these cracks, and withdraw them with the hot lava
adhering to them; I have brought one of these home for
you, as I believe such things amuse women and children.

Here I have said nothing about Rome, which I liked
much best of the three; but I have to go into town this
morning, so I will stop here for the present. . . .

21 March '98

. . . The end of the term is now in sight, and I am quite
ready for it; twelve weeks on end is not nice. I hope to
see a good many of the hedges green by the time the
holidays begin, as the spring is early in these parts. . . .

The only poem that I can find is this.

> I knew a Cappadocian
> Who fell into the Ocean:
> His mother came and took him out
> With tokens of emotion.
>
> She also had a daughter
> Who fell into the Water:
> At any rate she would have fallen
> If someone hadn't caught her.
>
> The second son went frantic
> And fell in the Atlantic:

His parent reached the spot too late
To check her offspring's antic.

Her grief was then terrific:
She fell in the Pacific,
Exclaiming with her latest breath
"I have been too prolific."

26 April 1898

. . . This is the first day of term; so, as the holidays are
over, I sit down to write a letter. I have to thank you
for two, one on my birthday and one later. You will
see that yours was not the only one I received on my
birthday: I believe you collect the epistles of this amiable
madman,[1] so I enclose this one for you. He must have discovered the date from a publication called *Who's Who*.

. . . Since I came back I have been having good walks
about the country to see things coming out in the sun-
shine, and I feel very well . . . I see from looking through
your letters that Eva is to be married to-morrow; so give
her my benediction.

Marriage, and the necessity of filling this sheet of
paper, remind me of one of my occasional poems, which
I may or may not have told you of before:

When Adam day by day
Woke up in Paradise,
He always used to say
'Oh, this is very nice.'

[1] An unknown correspondent, who wrote effusive letters to A.E.H. and
myself on our birthdays.

136

But Eve from scenes of bliss
Transported him for life.
The more I think of this
The more I beat my wife. . . .

(*Written on his return from Italy*)   27 Sept. 1900
. . . I suppose Milan is the least Italian town in Italy:
it considers itself the intellectual capital of the country,
and probably hopes to go to France when it dies.

Next to the Cathedral, the tramway seems to be the
thing on which the Milanese chiefly pride themselves.
The Cathedral, though one cannot call it good architecture if compared with French or English or even German
or the best Italian Gothic, is certainly impressive from
its mere size and magnificence and completeness, except
the west front, which has a mean effect and actually
looks small, thanks to the stupid Italian notion that the
proper outline for a west front is the same as that for a
dog-kennel . . . From other points of view the building
looks full its size, and indeed looks larger than St. Peter's
at Rome, though in fact it is much less. The ornament,
the pinnacles and statues and finials at the top, and the
niches at the side, looks rich at first, but it soon begins to
look poor: the recesses are shallow, the usual Italian fault,
the succession of upright lines is monotonous, and the
buttresses and pinnacles, though marble, look almost like
the iron work of a drawing-room fender, owing to the
thinness and stiffness of their ornament. The guide calls
your attention to the fact that no statues and no two

flowers of the carving are alike; but they might just as well be alike; they could not produce a greater effect of sameness. The inside is very dark, a fault on the right side, and so the defects in details do not trouble one much, and the general effect is fine.

The central aisle is half as high again as our highest, York and Westminster, and is quite English in its breadth, – not the narrow French proportion: there are double aisles on each side, the lowest of which I calculate are as high as the nave of Winchester. The clerestory is small, and there is no triforium, so fully three quarters of the height of the nave is merely pillars and arches: the pillars are crowned, not by capitals, but by octagonal stilts consisting of niches with statues in them, on the top of which the arches are perched: I suppose all this adds to the effect of height, but it is disproportional and fatigues the eyes: if you look straight before you there is only column after column: you cannot help looking up, and then there is nothing to see except the arches and the roof at a distance where you lose their outlines. . . .

2 October 1900

. . . I was in Milan on the day of Bresci's trial: at first I could not make out why the ends of all the streets round the Court of Justice were occupied by cavalry who let no wheeled traffic pass, but this accounted for it. I went to the top of the cathedral to see the view: the distance was not very clear, so that only the nearest Alps and Apennines were visible, not Mount Rosa. All round extends the plain of Lombardy as flat as a carpet, and very green with pollard trees and shrubs, red and white towns and towers here and there: the great Carthusian monastery and church of Pavia looks like a ship on the sea. Going from Milan to Venice at first you have merely this plain, cut up into small and narrow fields of Indian corn in all stages of growth (they call it Turkish corn, and to put matters straight they call a turkey an Indian fowl, poor benighted Papists); these fields are separated not by hedges, but by rows of small trees, black poplar, willow, and especially mulberry; they also plant the mulberry among the corn and in orchards by itself: they grow it for silk, not fruit. You cross many rivers, and at this time of the year you can tell by their condition where they come from: those which flow from the lakes have plenty of water, but those which have to rely on their own springs are merely brooks amidst broad white beds of sand and stones. When you are getting towards Brescia the Alps come down from the north to keep the railroad company: this part is very picturesque, the hills have towns and churches and forts and convents perched here and there; but there is a great lack of large trees: I believe there are not half a dozen large trees in Italy except in gardens and parks. The Lombardy poplar does not seem to be common in Lombardy: it grows badly, and they often lop it like a Worcestershire elm. . . .

Between Verona and Vicenza the Alps recede into the north again; the country is much like Lombardy, but the fields are larger and farms and towns seem fewer;

but every town and village, even more than in Lombardy, seems to have built itself a lofty brick bell-tower, which in Venetia generally has a short sort of spire on the top (you know the great campanile of St. Mark's at Venice): also the poplar becomes more frequent: people who live in very flat countries (Lincolnshire for instance) must have tall towers and such things to cheer them up. As the sun went down we came to what is called the dead lagoon, where the sea and land begin to mix, but there is more land than sea: the live lagoon, where there is more sea than land, is what Venice stands in. The scene was very dreary at that hour: pools and canals, and marshes all overgrown with that purple flower I sent you; and the last touch of mystery and desolation was provided by three large staring red tramcars about a quarter of a mile away which were being rapidly drawn, by one very small horse apiece, into the Adriatic sea. (I found afterwards that they go to a spot on the coast whence there is a steamer to Venice.) Then the railway runs out on to the water to Venice over a bridge two miles and a half long: Venice itself is not very well seen, and looks something like an English manufacturing town with the chimneys transformed into towers. Entering Venice itself, especially at nightfall, when most of the canals are empty, the first impression is its still-ness: you get a gondola at the landing place by the station, and are taken to the other end of the Grand Canal, where the hotels are, chiefly by short cuts through lesser canals: the Grand Canal is like an S. . . .

15 Oct. 1900

. . . I suppose I had better take the contents of Venice in the order of date. The first is the best: the Byzantine architecture as represented by the cathedral of St. Mark, which I should think is the most beautiful, though not the grandest, building in the world. It might be possible to erect in the Gothic style a more beautiful building, but I doubt if such a one exists . . . I used to go there nearly every day; but it would take years to exhaust it.

The few remaining palaces of the same architecture I did not think much of, though Ruskin cries them up a great deal. Of Gothic they had two sorts in Venice: one for the churches, very thin and poor, with naked red brick on the outside; another for their palaces, exceedingly rich and elegant, but rather timid and monotonous. Of this the Doge's palace is the great example: you know its stupid general design, like a clothes-horse with a blanket on it: I am bound to say the reality is better than the pictures, because one can see that the flat and tame upper half of it is composed of red and white marble, although the pattern is no better than you see on the cottages in the Stourbridge Road at Bromsgrove.

The painter best represented in Venice is that lurid and theatrical Tintoret, whom I avoid, and Paul Veronese, whom one soon sees enough of. There are surprisingly few Titians, though two of them are very fine and famous. The best paintings to my thinking are those of Giovanni Bellini, who belongs to the previous generation, and his pupil Cima de Conegliano, mostly

Madonnas and groups of saints; also two painters both called Bonifacio Veronese. . . .

My gondolier expressed a wish that he were your son. He wanted me to come to Venice next Christmas, and I explained that at Christmas I went to see you; and then he made this remark. The reason is, that if he were your son he would be well off and have no family to provide for: so at least he says. At present he has to earn a living for one wife, two sisters, one mother, one mother-in-law and half an uncle (who was once a champion oarsman and is now paralysed); which is pretty good for a young man of twenty-three who has had one eye kicked out by a horse. . . .

(Undated: written from Constantinople)

The ruins are not nearly so lofty as some of our English castles, but what strikes one is their immense extent and the loneliness around. Inside, the skirts of the city are thinly peopled, more market gardens than houses; outside, the country is rolling downs and grave-yards, with cultivation only here and there. A Turkish graveyard is a forest of cypresses with an undergrowth of tombstones, which dies much sooner than the trees; for a Turkish tombstone is no thicker and no broader than a plank, and is ill fixed in the ground, so that they soon begin to lean in all directions, and finally lie down flat upon the earth. The Jews bury their dead on the bare hillside under slabs: the great cemetery is west of Pera, above the Golden Horn, and makes the downs look as if they were sprinkled with large hailstones or coarse-grained salt.

Constantinople is famous for its sunsets, and I used to watch them from the western edge of the hill that Pera stands on, looking over the cypresses of what was once a graveyard but now contains only dust and dogs and is beginning to be built over. From here you look across the Golden Horn and west, where the sun goes under. The sky would be orange and the hillside of the city would be dark with a few lights coming out, and the Golden Horn would reflect the blue or grey of the upper sky; and as there was a new moon, the crescent used to come and hang itself appropriately over the mosque of Muhammad the Conqueror.

It was a great comfort to me not to have you with me in Constantinople: it would have been 'poor doggie!' every step of the way, and we should never have got a hundred yards from the hotel. They lie all about the streets and the pavement, mostly asleep, and almost all have got something the matter with them. They are extremely meek and inoffensive: Turkey is a country where dogs and women are kept in their proper place, and consequently are quite unlike the pampered and obstreperous animals we know under those names in England. The Turkish dog spends his life much like the English cat: he sleeps by day, and at night he grows melodious. He does not bark over his quarrels so much as English dogs do, and when he does bark it is sometimes rather like the quacking of a soprano duck; but he wails: whether he is winning or losing seems to make no difference, so dejected are his spirits. I soon got used to the noise, however, and it did not spoil my sleep. The people are very good in not treading on them, and so are the beasts of burden; but wheeled vehicles, which have got much commoner of late years, are less good to them, and the trams are not good to them at all. One night in the dark I trod on a dog lying exactly in the middle of the road: he squealed in a bitterly reproachful tone for a certain time; when he had finished, the next dog barked in an expostulatory manner for the same period, and then the incident was closed. Carts drawn by white oxen or by black buffaloes are pretty frequent in the streets; and once my carriage was stopped by a train of camels, but these are not common. The sheep, many of which are horned, have the whitest and prettiest wool I have ever seen. The Turks keep fighting rams as pets, and make matches between them: these lively creatures may sometimes be met in the streets, invading the greengrocers' shops and butting at the boys, who catch them by the horns.

The population is very mixed, and largely descended from kidnapped Christians. Pure Turks are rather rare, Greeks and Armenians common: a man is an Armenian when his nose is like this �ↄ. I have come across the handsomest faces I ever saw: their figures are not so good. Some of the Greeks make you rub your eyes; their features and complexions are more like pictures than realities: though the women unfortunately bleach themselves by keeping out the sun. The Turks, when they are good looking, I like even better; there is an aquiline type like the English aristocracy very much improved: if I could send you the photograph of a young man who rowed me to the Sweet Waters of Asia, and asked you to guess his name, you would instantly reply 'Aubrey de Vere Plantagenet'. But unless they take to outdoor work they get fat at an early age. . . .

(*Fragments of a subsequent letter: the rest is missing*)

. . . It is the great place to see the view from, as it commands the whole city, and shows you parts of the Bosphorus and Golden Horn and Sea of Marmora and the coast of Asia opposite. It is now used as a watch-tower for fires, which are common and dangerous in a city mostly built of wood. The watchmen pace round and look out of the eight windows continually for smoke or fire; then they signal by hanging out a flag by day or a lamp by night from the window which looks towards the fire, and this sign is seen by all the fire-stations. The fire-engines then go to the spot indicated and gaze at the conflagration: if the owner of the property likes to hire them, they will put out the fire for him, but not otherwise.

From letters to his sister, Mrs. E. W. Symons. These letters always began 'My dear Kate', and were signed 'Your affectionate brother A. E. Housman'.

Trinity College,
Cambridge.
30 Dec. 1911.

*(Written shortly after his appointment as Kennedy Pro-
fessor of Latin)*

. . . I am staying here through the vacation as I am
seeing a book through the press and found that I could
not do much at it during the term. Being conscientious,
I took a good deal of time to prepare my lectures; and
being a new-comer, I was much asked out to dinner.
People here are very hospitable and friendly. The
attendance at my lectures was from 20 to 30 (which,
though not large, is from 20 to 30 times greater than the
attendance at my predecessor's), several of whom were
lecturers themselves. I believe the lectures are considered
good (as indeed they are).

I don't know that the climate exactly suits me, and
probably I have drunk too much port at College Feasts;
but I am not feeling stupid, which is the great thing.

The twins of Mrs. Martin of Hereford called on me the
other day, when they were up for scholarships. They
were as fluent and self-possessed as ever, and conversed
affably on subjects which they thought likely to interest
me. I see that each got a scholarship or exhibition,
though only for £40, Cambridge being less munificent
than Oxford. . . .

3 Oct. 1920

. . . Well, I flew there[1] and back all right, and am never going by any other route in future. Surrey from overhead is delightful, Kent and France less interesting, the Channel disappointing, because on both days there was too much mist to let both shores be seen at once. It was rather windy, and the machine sometimes imitated a ship at sea (though that is due to differing densities of atmosphere and not to wind) but not in a very life-like manner. Members of your unhappy sex were sick, however. The noise is great, and I alighted rather deaf, not having stuffed my ears with the cotton-wool provided. Nor did I put on the life-belt which they oblige one to take. To avoid crossing the 60 miles of sea which a straight flight would involve, they go from Croydon to Hythe, Hythe to Boulogne, Boulogne to Paris. You are in the air 2½ hours: from Leicester Square to your hotel in Paris you take little more than four; though on the return journey we were 2 hours late in starting because the machine required repairs, having been damaged on the previous day by a passenger who butted his head through the window to be sick. My chief trouble is that what I now want is no longer a motor and a chauffeur but an aeroplane and a tame pilot, which I suppose are more expensive. The weather in France was beautiful, though I read of storms in London. Unfortunately I got poisoned at a restaurant and was out of action for the best part of two days. Pray why should the manager of W. H.

[1] Paris.

147

Smith's establishment in Paris want to know if you are my sister? It was not me he asked, but Grant Richards; and twice. . . .

26 March 1923

. . . Thanks for your letter on my birthday with its enclosures. I may as well sit down at once and answer it, not being much good for anything else. For the last three weeks I have been about as ill as I ever have been in the course of a fairly healthy life, with boils on the neck and a carbuncle on the back; though I daresay poor Basil has often been worse. The doctor says I am better to-day, and I think perhaps I am.

It is very pleasant to see how happy and active Jerry[1] is: he seems to have found his vocation. I don't exactly know what his office is, nor whereabouts he is in the large province of Bengal: not far from Calcutta apparently.

I had meant to spend this vacation in interesting work: now, as soon as I can get out, I shall probably have to waste the rest of it at the seaside.

I receive, though I do not wish to, the *Weekly West-minster* in which my verses are translated. The prize copy of Greek elegiacs had a false quantity in the second line: I did not read on to see if there were more. . . .

[1] His nephew, N. V. H. Symons.

Hotel Continental

Paris

18 Aug. 1923

. . . Your letter reached me here yesterday on my return from a motor tour of a fortnight in Britanny. The weather has been most obsequious; blazing hot all the time while motor-travel could temper it, and turning cool now that heat would be a nuisance. Britanny is much less wild than I supposed, and much like parts of England, the neighbourhood of Midhurst for instance, though not so hilly. The churches and cathedrals are better than I had any idea of, and extraordinarily numerous. You would be more interested in the varieties of the female head-dress, which is different for every district. Finisterre is an impressive headland, and provided a fine sunset, and also a Scotch mist. The coast scenery in general is extraordinarily superior to the English in its mixture of land and water, and the islands and rocks. Carnac is almost as unimpressive as Stonehenge.

Together with your letter I have one from some photographers, who say that they are taking, 'for press purposes', photographs of ladies and gentlemen who are in the habit of flying between London and Paris, and they want to take mine, as they 'understand that I have also had that distinction'. I was delayed a day because the weather of July 31 was too dangerous for the aeroplane to start; but on August 1 I had the best voyage I have ever had. We crossed the Channel 7000 feet high, higher than the piles of clouds which lay over both shores, and both coasts were visible at once, which I have not found before. . . .

Trinity College
Cambridge
3 Jan. 1924

. . . This post-card comes in the nick of time to make me answer your letter. I am quite well now, except for a slight goutiness; but that is chronic, my friends, so do not grieve for me. I have been here since I came back from Britanny at the end of August, except that a month ago I went to Oxford to read a paper and stayed a week-end with the Poet Laureate on the top of Boars Hill there. He is an amazing old man: at 79 he gets up at 5 in the morning, lights his own fire and makes his coffee, and does a lot of work before breakfast. He has a large number of correct opinions, and is delighted when he finds that I have them too, and shakes hands with me when I say that the Nuns' Priest's Tale is Chaucer's best poem, and that civilization without slavery is impossible. . . .

2 June 1926

. . . I should write to tell you that I am going abroad on Saturday for a fortnight or three weeks: first on a short visit to Venice, where my poor gondolier says he is dying and wants to see me again, and then to Paris. . . .

23 June 1926

I got back safe yesterday, after three days' beautiful weather in Venice and a very dull time in Paris till just the last. My gondolier was looking pretty well, as warmth suits him, but he is quite unable to row and gets out of breath if he goes up many stairs. He is being sent by the municipal authorities for another three months' treatment in hospital, as they still find bacilli in his blood, and I suppose he will go steadily down hill. I was surprised to find what pleasure it gave me to be in Venice again. It was like coming home, when sounds and smells which one had forgotten stole upon one's senses; and certainly there is no place like it in the world: everything there is better in reality than in memory. I first saw it on a romantic evening after sunset in 1900, and I left it on a sunshiny morning, and I shall not go there again. . . .

31 March 1935

. . . As to my precious health, about six weeks ago I had a turn of not being able to sleep lying down, and consequently four sleepless nights in succession. That soon passed away, but the result is that I am less well than I have been since I came back from France last September, in point of strength for walking and studying, and also I have not much appetite. However, owing I suppose to the magic of your letter on my birthday, I have been walking much more strongly since that date.

I do not much mind things which properly belong to old age, but the nervous annoyance every morning, and undue sensitiveness to noises which I used not to mind, are extras, and do not show any sign of leaving off. My work is no tax on me, except that I have had to write the University's Address to the King on this so-called jubilee, which was a worry, though there was no reason why it should be. I am very sorry that you have had trouble with your eyes, a thing which I should not like at all; and it is lucky that you could find some solace in wireless. . . .

19 July 1935

. . . It was very pleasant to see you again, and I was glad that we were able to manage it, and in such pleasant circumstances. Jeannie's[1] recovery seems miraculous, and except that she does not come down to breakfast I can see no difference between now and two years ago.

I don't think I ever congratulated you on all the news in your last letter, such as the King's favouritism towards your three sons, and the demand for your historical work in America.

I enclose a copy of the address to the King which you wanted to see. I have been complimented to an absurd extent, but not enough to repay me for the bother of composing it. . . .

[1] His sister-in-law.

From letters to his brother Basil, and to his sister-in-law,
Jeannie Housman

29 Dec. 1927

. . . I have had a terrible shock from a telegram to-day from a London fishmonger. All the native oysters have been torn from their beds by tempest, and I shall have to eat the New Year in on Dutch. For me it therefore opens gloomily, but I hope that you and Jeannie will not find it saddened by any such calamity.

I had a visit not long ago from Clarence Darrow, the great American barrister for defending murderers. He had only a few days in England, but he could not return home without seeing me, because he had so often used my poems to rescue his clients from the electric chair. Loeb and Leopold owe their life sentence partly to me; and he gave me a copy of his speech, in which, sure enough, two of my pieces are misquoted.

Don't trouble to acknowledge what my banker sends to yours at the New Year, – unless he doesn't, as the Irishman would say. . . .

30 Dec. 1929

. . . This is to wish you and Basil a happy New Year, and to thank you for your two last letters. . . .

To-morrow night I shall be taking steps to keep up my health and strength in 1930 by eating any amount of oysters up to 4 doz. and drinking all the stout required to wash them down. After which, as it says in the

advertisement of Mrs. Winslow's soothing syrup, 'the dear little darling wakes up as bright as a button.'

Laurence was here some weeks ago, engaged in some villainy connected with the League of Nations. Of course I did not go to hear him, but he looked in on me, and seemed very well. . . .

I have composed no poem this year, but as Basil is fond of my warblings I have put together some scraps written at various times. . . .

3 Dec. 1934

. . . Here is December, bringing round the sad time when we lost Basil,[1] but bringing also this year to me in a letter from Kate the good news that you are wonderfully better in health and have kicked your nurse out of doors. I do beg you to keep it up and not to be weary in well doing. The winter, thus far, is being quite nice to invalids, of whom, however, we have rather a large number here among my friends and acquaintances. One of my best boon-companions died a few months ago, and apparently spoke so much and so well of me in his last illness that his nurse has written to me to engage herself for my death-bed. People, however, are always telling me that I look exceedingly well; so that, I fear, must be a pleasure deferred. . . .

11 Dec. 1935

. . . I was very glad to get your long and early Christmas letter, with the news, among other things, that your

---

[1] December 1st, 1932.

family is soon to indulge again in its favourite recreation of marriage. I hope the young couple will be happy and will find some means of livelihood.

My present rooms are the warmest and cosiest that could be well imagined; and the bath-room, which has been equipped by the College, is the admiration and envy of all beholders. I myself walk very feebly and do not sleep very well, and my breathing is apt to be trouble-some; but the comforts around me make me more cheer-ful than I should otherwise be. I can get through all the work that is required of me, and I go out to dinner when invited. One of the medicines I am taking is champagne, which however is not a wine I am very fond of. . . .

31 Jan. 1936

. . . I am sorry to hear that you have been ill and laid up, and I hope your recovery is proceeding as it should. As you say nothing of Grace I suppose that she is despising us both and exulting in good health. When your letter reached me I had strength to read it but not to answer it; and this is one of many pieces of correspondence which I am trying to overtake. In several respects I am much more comfortable and cheerful than when I went into the nursing home at Christmas, but my physical weakness (chiefly due I suppose to lying so long in bed) is extreme and very vexatious; and next to walking, writing seems to be what tires me most. On the other hand my lectures are no trouble. Some shadow is cast over the pleasure with which I look forward to visiting you in the summer

by perplexity how I am to manage your stairs. True, there are not 44 of them, but they are precipitous; and the days when I used to take them two at a time are not likely to return . . . .

From letters to Laurence Housman, 1894-1936, addressed always to 'My dear Laurence', and signed, 'Your affectionate brother A. E. Housman'

Byron Cottage, North Road
Highgate
14 Dec. 1894

I have got your poems into what seems to me a rough order of merit. *Love-bound Time* I think is the most original, and it is very well written and quite as lucid as one can expect; though I rather doubt if the English language will allow the stanza beginning 'Beauty may to beauty err' to mean anything in particular: however, it sounds nice. *Prisoner of Carisbrooke* ought certainly to be included, as it has more root in earth than most of its author's lays, and occupies the proud position of distinctly meaning something from beginning to end: also I think it good in itself, though 'well-water'[1] is rather neiges d'antan. *The Three Kings* is very good verse, except the end of the 12th stanza and the 2nd line of the 13th; in the 14th too I don't like 'this tells', though I am afraid that cannot be altered without sacri-

---

[1] Meaning with the accent, for the sake of rhyme, on the last syllable.

ficing 'Earth, Earth, Earth', on which you have probably set your young affections. Poems on pictures seem
to me an illegitimate genre, but *Autumn Leaves* is a
favourable specimen. . . . 'At the undarkening of
days' might be made into something, but it would take
a lot of making: at present it is not only so obscure as to
suggest that the poet does not quite know what he would
be at, but fearfully untidy into the bargain: for instance,
one cannot put an accent on the first syllable of 'interro-
gation'; and if 'hopen' means 'holpen' it does not
rhyme with 'open'. I doubt if *The Sleep of the Gods*
signifies much. *Blind Fortune* and *The King's Gifts* I
should decidedly leave out, and, for my own part, the
remaining pieces; these show a certain proficiency, in a
certain style, which shall wax old as doth a garment: still,
I daresay some will admire them: your Scotch friend very
likely, who draws large cats. I would die many deaths
rather than use such words as 'a-croon' and 'a-saw';
but that holy man St. Jerome very truly observes 'nemo
tam imperitus scriptor est qui lectorem non inveniat
similem sui' (the worst hand at writing in the world is
sure to find some reader of his own kidney).

What makes many of your poems more obscure than
they need be is that you do not put yourself in the
reader's place and consider how, and at what stage, that
man of sorrows is to find out what it is all about. You
are behind the scenes and know all the data; but he
knows only what you tell him. It appears from the
alternative titles *Heart's bane* and *Little Death* that in

writing that precious croon you had in your head some meaning of which you did not suffer a single drop to escape into what you wrote: you treat us as Nebuchadnezzar did the Chaldeans, and expect us to find out the dream as well as the interpretation. That is the worst instance; but there are others where throughout the first half of a poem the hapless reader is clawing the air for a clue and has not enough breath in his body to admire anything you show him. Take *The Stolen Mermaid*: I was some time in discovering who was talking, whether it was the stolen mermaid or the robbed merman. There matters might be made clearer by altering the crabbed lines 'O, heart to captive be', etc., into something like 'This land-bound heart of me Hears sound its mother-sea', only better expressed I hope. In *The Great Ride*, to begin with, you had better add place as well as date to the title, or the allusion may easily be missed. You start off 'Where the merciful waters *rolled*': the reader sees the past tense, and instead of thinking of the heavenly Jordan, as you want him to, he is off to Abana and Pharphar, rivers of Damascus, and expects to hear you tell him about some historical crossing of a river where a lot of people were killed: all which you would avoid by saying '*roll*'. Further: how soon do you imagine your victim will find out that you are talking about horses? Not until the thirteenth of these long lines, unless he is such a prodigy of intelligence and good will as I am: there you mention 'hoofs', and he has to read the thirteen lines over again. 'Flank' in line six is not enough: Swinburne's women have flanks. And as line six is at present a foot too short I advise you to introduce hoofs into it; or tails?

Now I will go through some details. You will find here and there some marginal suggestions in pencil which may help to shew in what direction I think improvements might be made. . . .

[Then follow a number of small corrections of rhymes, single words, and punctuation.]

The Fire Worshippers is surely a very bad title and rather helps to confuse. 'Man, Truth, and Beauty' would be, not good I daresay, but better. 'Bowels': if terrific sublimity is what you are after, say 'guts'; which has the further advantage of being one syllable, and not two, like 'bowels', though I am aware that Aytoun rhymes the latter with 'howls'. But nobody rent Prometheus' bowels that I know of, so I should say 'side' like an ordinary creature. '*Speak the word* which spells' will suggest d-o-g, c-a-t, etc. The first two lines of the fourth stanza I can't very well advise about, not knowing what they mean.

The Stolen Mermaid. 'To the bay's *caves*' is where the upward not the downward tide would go. 'If, ah, but if' displays with almost cynical candour its mission to rhyme with 'cliff'. It might be 'hill' and 'if still, if still'. . . .

Under the Rose I call a bad title; because I suppose you don't mean it to signify *Clandestinely*, yet how can the reader think anything else? It strikes me too that, as you tell the tale, the hero gets his roses cheap, for we don't hear that he did give much mirth to earth: apparently he merely lay under the rose and chuckled, and earth said 'how that boy is enjoying himself!'

The Great Ride. 'in *tragic* accord'. I suspect Miss A. Mary F. Robinson began with *tragic*: then in the fulness of time she got to *insensate*: be warned and pause. What are 'gods of Mammon'? I thought Mammon was a god, since Spenser and Milton: in the other sense the newspapers have got it. . . .

The Sleep of the Gods. Does one put one's head either to one's own heart or to another person's (for it is not clear which this god did) in order to hear the beat of feet? The last stanza of this poem is one of your triumphs of obscurity. I have come to the conclusion, which may be wrong, that the two last lines are uttered by Deep to Deep, and not sung by the gods, because the pronoun 'their' appears to require this interpretation; but if so, what black inhumanity on your part not to say 'whispered' or the like instead of 'trembled'.

Heart's bane alias *Little Death* alias *White Rabbits*: If you print this, better *not* employ the last title, but keep your rabbits for an agreeable surprise in the last verse.

I daresay I have left out some things I meant to say, but here is the paper at an end. . . .

31 March 1895

. . . I think Le Gallienne has picked out the four or five best. *The Blue Eyes of Margret* would be as good as any, if the words 'while heart's memories met' conveyed any meaning, which to me they don't; and I think the poem would gain if they vanished ... *Lord Paramount* is superior in execution to anything I have seen of yours; though I think I said before that men were not created to write poems about pictures. *The Keepsake*, with its beautiful moral lesson, is clever and striking; though your Muse is apt perhaps to preoccupy herself unduly with the phenomena of gestation. *The Queen's Bees* is about as good in another way; but on the last page the two lines about fashion and passion are evidently not meant literally: then how in the world are they meant? and their phraseology is precious cheap. I don't know if it wouldn't improve the poem to run on straight from 'a poor man's way' to 'Then would I give'. Another point: do you really know what the Queen did to the poor man? If she bent him flat, as you said at first, that explains his resentment, though it sounds rather comic; but in the second version she gives him nothing to cry about. *The Cornkeeper* may go along with these. I don't care for any of the others I now see for the first time. I return the list you sent of Le Gallienne's rejections, etc.: I have put a cipher to what I think should be left out and underlined what I think should be printed: where I have put no mark I have no definite opinion. As to *The Great Ride*, Le Gallienne truly says that it is in another key than the rest, but I don't know if that is altogether an objection: it may find its way to hearts from which White Rabbits run off like water from a duck's back. Its faults seem to me rather its length, and its theme, which I don't think really very well suited to poetry.

A few details.

The Keepsake. 'She waits by the windowsill and whistles.' Do you think so, Jim? The accomplishment is rare among women. . . .

The Bleeding Arras. This fails to impress, all the more because of the evident intention to impress. By the way, arras, embarrass and harass are brazen effrontery. . . .

The House of Birth. This is less indecent than Rossetti and less comical than W. E. Henley, but that is all I can say for it.

The Two Debtors. I do not understand this, and perhaps that is why I think it perfectly odious.

King B's Daughter. Nor this; but that may be the fault of my ignorance in not knowing who this monarch was.[1]

The Dedication is pretty, especially the end of the second verse. In some places it lumbers by reason of having heavy syllables where light ones ought to be: 'Is each bird that *here* sings', 'Where *dim* lights and *dark* shadows belong *Hangs* the arras of song'. The beginning of the last verse I think is doggerel, especially the third line; and the third stanza is weak except at the end. But the chief objection is not merely the Swinburnian style of the whole but the fact that Swinburne has twice used almost this same metre for a dedication. . . .

[1] Bagdemagus (Malory's *Morte D'Arthur*).

(On the publication of 'A Shropshire Lad')

27 April '96

. . . Why am I being reviewed in semi-religious papers like the *New Age* and the *British Weekly*? and how does that sort of literature find its way to Marloes Road? and where do you suppose did the *British Weekly* learn my antecedents?

There is rather a good notice in last week's *Sketch*.

I thought the *New Age* review very nice, except the first paragraph disparaging the other chaps.

Kate writes to say that she likes the verse better than the sentiments. The sentiments, she then goes on to say, appear to be taken from the book of Ecclesiastes. To prefer my versification to the sentiments of the Holy Ghost is decidedly flattering, but strikes me as a trifle impious. . . .

26 Sept. '96

. . . I have *Green Arras* and thank you very much for it. Of the poems I think I have seen all but one or two before. Of the illustrations I like *The Queen's Bees* the best, with its distant view and its kidney bean sticks: the scarecrow is full of life and is perhaps the best of your wind-blown pillow-cases to date; and the figure in the foreground wins upon one when one realises that what one at first took for his nose is really and truly his chin. *The Corn-keeper* looks much better than it did in *Atalanta*. The central or principal figure in *The House-builders* strikes me as very good indeed, if his right arm were a trifle shorter; but if I were the employer of those bricklayers I should take care to pay them by the piece and not by the day.

I am much disappointed to find no illustration to *White Rabbits*. I have attempted to supply this deficiency and I enclose the result. You will see that I have had some difficulty with the young lady's arm; and the gentleman is not quite as tall as I could have wished. The moon (together with the weather-vanes and everything else which I could not draw) is behind the spectator, which accounts for the vivid illumination of the principal figures. You may remark that the rabbits are not running: true; but they have been running, and they are just going to begin again.

The other enclosure is not one of my finished works: I should hardly call it more than a sketch. It depicts the meeting at the end of *The Keepsake*.

I think I would have put either *The Keepsake* or else *The Queen's Bees* nearer the beginning of the volume, as these are the two pieces I should expect to attract most attention; and *The Comforters* does not strike me as a very ingratiating poem to put so early. Otherwise I think the arrangement is good. . . .

I think you will probably be able to congratulate yourself on having brought out this autumn at the Bodley Head a much better book than Davidson, if the whole of his *New Ballads* are at all like those he has been publishing in the magazines. Not that this is a very lofty compliment. . . .

5 Oct. 1896

. . . I was in Bridgnorth for several hours. In the churchyard there I remembered having heard our mother describe it and the steps up to it, which I had absolutely forgotten for more than 25 years.

I ascertained by looking down from Wenlock Edge that Hughley Church could not have much of a steeple. But as I had already composed the poem and could not invent another name that sounded so nice, I could only deplore that the church at Hughley should follow the bad example of the Church at Brou, which persists in standing on a plain after Matthew Arnold has said that it stands among mountains. I thought of putting a note to say that Hughley was only a name, but then I thought that would merely disturb the reader. I did not apprehend that the faithful would be making pilgrimages to these holy places.

Morris dead! now Swinburne will have something to write about. He wrote 12 epicediums on P. B. Marston, so Morris ought to be good for at least 144.

Reading your poems in print I was a good deal struck by *Gammer Garu*, which I don't remember noticing much in manuscript. The last stanza is really quite beautiful.

A new firm of publishers has written to me proposing to publish 'the successor' of *A.S.L.* But as they don't also offer to write it, I have had to put them off. . . .

4 Dec. 1896

. . . There has been no notice in the *Bookman* yet. I feel sure you are wrong in thinking that A. M. stands for Mrs. Meynell; partly because of the style, which is neither sufficiently correct nor sufficiently pretentious, and partly because the sub-editor's name is A. Macdonnell.

I have been reading your latest work,[1] – probably by this time it is not your latest work, but I can't read as fast as you write. What I chiefly admire in your stories, here as on previous occasions, is the ingenuity of the plan: this particularly applies to *The King's Evil*, which I thought a good deal the best of this set. The pieces of poetry interspersed seem to me better in point of diction than any in *Green Arras*. The sentiments are a bit lurid. 'Long through the night', 'Amid this grave-strewn', and 'You the dear trouble' struck me as the best; but there are a number of good verses in the others. . . .

12 May 1897

. . . There is a notice of *Gods and their Makers* in last week's *Athenaeum*: I don't know if it is depreciatory enough to suit your taste.

George Darley was the writer of the excellent sham 17th century song 'It is not beauty I demand' which Palgrave printed as genuine in the 2nd part of the *Golden Treasury*. Because it was so good I read another thing of his, a sort of fairy drama whose name I forget,

[1] *All-Fellows.*

and was disappointed with it and read no more. But the
piece you quote about the sea is capital. He was also the
chief praiser of Beddoes' first play, and a great detester of
Byron's versification when it was all the vogue.

The sea is a subject by no means exhausted. I have
somewhere a poem which directs attention to one of its
most striking characteristics, which hardly any of the
poets seem to have observed. They call it salt and blue
and deep and dark and so on; but they never make such
profoundly true reflexions as the following:

> O billows bounding far,
> How wet, how wet ye are!
>
> When first my gaze ye met
> I said 'Those waves are wet'.
>
> I said it, and am quite
> Convinced that I was right.
>
> Who saith that ye are dry?
> I give that man the lie.
>
> Thy wetness, O thou sea,
> Is wonderful to me.
>
> It agitates my heart,
> To think how wet thou art.
>
> No object I have met
> Is more profoundly wet.

Methinks 'twere vain to try,
O sea, to wipe thee dry.

I therefore will refrain.
Farewell, thou humid main.

Farewell, thou irreligious writer. . . .

[As Editor of *The Venture* I had asked A.E.H. for a contribution; and had suggested an article on Coventry Patmore. ' 'Tis mute, the word they went to hear' was the poem I chose.]

9 August 1903

. . . To write a paper on Patmore would be an awful job, especially in the holidays, so I send you two poems, of which you can print whichever you think the least imperfect.

I hope you won't succeed in getting anything from Meredith, as I am a respectable character, and do not care to be seen in the company of galvanised corpses. By this time he stinketh: for he hath been dead twenty years. . . .

7 Feb. 1907

. . . I have induced Dr. Morris to tell me, on condition that Mamma does not hear that he told, the amount of his bill for last year. It is about £70.0.0; and I want to find out, if possible, what this will mean to Mamma. I have no clear notion of what her income is and what margin it generally leaves her; and perhaps you or Clemence can give me some notion. I am anxious to prevent her from feeling any severe pinch for the bill, but on the other hand I don't want to be extravagant or ostentatious; so if you can help me to judge what I should give her in order to effect these two ends I should be much obliged.

Your bad behaviour in the theatre[1] I first heard of from your letters which were read to me at Hereford; I had seen nothing in the papers. I see the play is now taken off, but I suppose it will go into the provinces.

Rothenstein has made me a present of one of his three portraits of me. Perhaps when the weather is warmer and the spring more advanced you and Clemence will come out here and look at it. . . .

30 April 1907

. . . I don't at all want to contribute to Mrs. Bland's[2] publication. I contributed to *The Venture* only because you were the editor. I suppose she already knows that I am morose and unamiable, and will not experience any sudden or agonising shock. . . .

17 Feb. 1908

. . . I should be very glad to look through your selections. Did I ever say anything abusive about *Spikenard*?[3] I think on the whole it is about the cleverest of your poetry books. . . .

---

[1] The *Vicar of Wakefield* affair, told of in *The Unexpected Years*.
[2] E. Nesbit.
[3] He had described it as 'nonsense verse'.

So overpowering is your celebrity that I have just received an official letter from my own college addressed to 'Professor L. Housman'. . . .

(This letter refers to my 'Selected Poems')

1 March 1908

. . . With your inclusions from *Spikenard* I agree, except that I have very decidedly struck out one. In the other books I have not actually struck out anything (except once) and have even made one or two additions, which I think quite as good as the average of the inclusions. The pieces which I think your best, apart from *Spikenard*, are, in *Rue*, 'Long through the night', 'Amid this grave-strewn', 'What know ye of', and 'Dark to its nest'; in *Mendicant Rhymes*, *The Settlers*; and in *The Little Land*, *The Elfin Bride*: so I think these should in any case go in. *Mendicant Rhymes* itself, though rather obscure and un-tidy, is decidedly pretty, but the stanza where 'Chloe' rhymes to 'Evoe' would have to be altered, because Evoe is a word of two syllables, εὐοῖ, and the *oe* is a diphthong, and you might put two million dots on the top of it instead of two without changing its length. Speaking generally, I think the inclusions at present too many and too monotonous: I should not put in all the sonnets of *The Little Land* (sonnets stodge up a book more than anything, even blank verse), nor so much of *Rue*. The strong point of your poetry seems to me to be a lively fancy: you seem rather to value the pieces on account of thoughts or emotions which suggested them, without enough considering whether they are really reproduced in the words. Thus 'Across these barren clods' is much more attractive and intelligible to a reader than a great deal of its surroundings, which you prefer; and similarly *A Garden Enclosed* is more successful than *The Man in Possession*, though I don't understand 'life's a fault' in the last verse. *The New Orpheus* I should call too long, and by no means so good in its way as *Advocatus Diaboli*, though this wants making clearer and neater in parts.

I should be glad to look over the text when the selections are made, especially as you have a way of treating words like 'Messiah' and 'royal' as if they were a syllable shorter than they are, – possibly in the vain hope of making amends for 'Evoë'. . . .

27 June 1908

. . . I enjoyed parts of your play[1] very much, especially the first transformation of the picture, which was so effective that I think the act ought to have ended there. Olangtsi is very good and very well acted, and Mee Mee too is quite nice, and the Jews, especially the opulent one, are amusing. The acting of the students on the other hand, especially their voices and intonation, I thought almost the worst I had ever come across; and the words they have to say and sing seem to me to contain a good deal of your wet wit. And then there is the infernal music. Theatres are beginning to exhibit notices asking ladies to remove their hats; my patronage shall be

[1] *The Chinese Lantern.*

171

bestowed on the theatre which goes a step further and requests the orchestra to be silent. The sleep-walking scene ought to have been good; but it left me faint and weak from the effort of straining to hear the human voice through the uproar of pussy's bowels.

Rothenstein asked me to express to you his great pleasure and admiration. He also explained to me the moral; which is that if one wants to be a great artist one must be *absorbed* in a work of art. He very politely assumed that I saw it myself; but alas, I did not.

Both Millington and George Fletcher want to see me at the Bromsgrove dinner on the 8th, so I am going; but I have announced to Bunting that I shall not make a speech.

I read an article on your work by a most affected writer in a magazine whose name I forget, though I have got it in the next room; and I have sufficient artistic taste to be aware that the drawing of a lady and a tortoise is good. About the *Night* I should not have felt sure; not that I have anything against it. . . .

3 Nov. 1908

. . . On page 11[1] 'when first knighted' sounds very prosy, though I don't think my suggestion much better, as it is ambiguous. I have not found much else to note. The pieces on pp. 18 and 28 are really quite nice: I don't remember noticing them before.

[1] Of *Selected Poems*.

I was at Cambridge a week or two ago, and met a lady who asked if I were the author of *Gods and their Makers*. Always honest, I owned that I was not: I said I was his brother. 'Oh, well,' said she, 'that's the next best thing.' It appears that the work is a household word with them: they have a dog or a cat called after one of your divinities. . . .

8 Nov. 1908

. . . The changes in *Advocatus Diaboli* are very judicious.

The line on p. 52 is as bad as ever. I think you should try what you can do with *default* or *assault*; for I am afraid that salt and malt and cobalt are no good. There is however a kind of stiff clay called gault, in which I daresay sepulchres are sometimes dug.

On p. 71, last line but one, I should restore the old reading, because it is not good to have two lines with their last halves so much on the same model as *the pangs he bore* and *the wound he wore*.

The misprint on p. 101 is eloquent of the printer's cockney pronunciation. . . .

16 Dec. 1908

. . . Thanks for your poems. I suppose if I say anything in praise of the cover and get-up you will detect insinuations as to the contents, so I had better not. . . .

30 Jan. 1911

. . . I thank you both for your congratulations.[1] It is not by any means certain that I could have secured the Oxford chair by waiting for it; and on the whole I think I prefer Cambridge.

I spent one of my hard-earned half-crowns on the *English Review* containing the trial-scene of your play:[2] it interested me, but I did not think it would interest most people, without the Censor's assistance.

Disraeli visited the villa where your heroine resided in Italy, soon after the trial. Its decorations, he says, were of such a character that it was painful to view them in company with a lady. The local Italians regarded the tumult in London as a great joke. . . .

9 June 1910

. . . I would rather not sign your memorial;[3] chiefly because I don't think that writers as a class are particularly qualified to give advice on the question; and moreover it is certain to be signed by Galsworthy and Hewlett and everyone I cannot abide. Also I cannot say that 'the solution of this question appears to me to be urgent'. Even if I were actually in favour of woman suffrage in the abstract, I think I should like to see some other and less precious country try it first: America for instance, where the solution ought to be just as urgent as here.

Thanks for the pamphlet. I see you have another just

---

[1] On his appointment to the Kennedy Chair of Latin.
[2] *Pains and Penalties.*
[3] A declaration by authors in favour of Woman Suffrage.

published, but as that costs 6d. I recognise that it is my duty to buy it; which indeed I am quite able to do, as your literary activity has fallen off of late, and my finances are recovering from the strain it used to put on them.

Love to Clemence: I hope she has read, or will read, *Ann Veronica* (the prison scenes). . . .

27 April 1911

. . . This is to say that I am not coming to hear your seditious play, and I shall not make any attempt to see you, as your time will probably be taken up with more whole-hearted admirers. For the same reason I suppose you will not be coming to see me, though I shall be glad to see you if you do. . . .

11 June 1911

. . . Although I had very few official duties during the Cambridge term I was much occupied with social duties, which are a deal worse, and either from the climate or the heat was generally tired when I was not occupied, so that I have not thanked you for the proofs of your play. It interested me, but I should not have thought it would interest most people, nor be effective on the stage. However, everyone who heard it was loud in praise of your reading, and apparently swallowed Caroline whole.

An undergraduate came to me to get your address, which I gave him, after exacting assurances that he was not bent on avenging the glorious house of Hanover. . . .

10 Oct. 1913

. . . An American ecclesiastic was here the other day, who asked to be presented to me, and from whom I gathered that his favourite work would be *A Shropshire Lad*, but for the existence of that fascinating story, *The Were Wolf*, which, again, would be his favourite work, but for the existence of the most brilliant political satire ever written, *King John of Jingalo*.

10 Feb. 1917

. . . Thanks for your *Return of Alcestis*, which as a whole I do not very much admire, in spite of a good many good lines. On the other hand the last work of yours that I read, *The Royal Runaway*, I thought even better than *John of Jingalo*, at least till the revolution came, which I did not much believe in.

I was at Eton last Sunday and came across two boys, the sons of suffragists named Harben living somewhere near, to whom on one occasion in a closed carriage you recited reams of poetry which they supposed to be your own; but the only fragment which they could repeat was mine. It says a great deal for your conversational ascendancy that the incident took place, for in any other company those two boys would do the talking and not the listening. . . .

4 Dec. 1919

. . . I have not thanked you as I should for the trilogy[1] you sent me on Nov. 17, but I have not been able to read

[1] *The Wheel.*

it through at leisure till lately. You do not need to be told that there is a good deal to admire in it; and there are passages, such as the last four lines, which I like very much. But as to the style in general I cannot do better than copy out a couple of sentences from a review of mine: 'In the sixties it seemed indeed as if there had arisen a band of writers to launch poetry on a new career; but time showed that they were cruising in a backwater, not finding a channel for the main stream, and in twenty years all heart had gone out of the enterprise. The fashions of that interlude are already so antique that Mr. Gilbert Murray can adapt them for his rendering of Euripides; and they now receive academic approbation, which is the second death.' As to the moral rules incumbent on gods and men, they alter as time goes on, but do not improve, though each age in succession thinks its own rules right. My own sense of propriety however is not so much offended by anything you have taken from the ancient story as by your scuttling Alcestis at Scapa Flow on p. 74.

I hear from Kate that you are leaving for America on the 30th, and I wish you a pleasant and prosperous tour. If they pay you in dollars you ought to come back rich. . . .

21 Sept. 1920

. . . That is all right. I hope that by fair means and foul together you despoiled America of a great deal of its appreciated coinage.

I have just flown to Paris and back, and am never

going by any other route, until they build the Channel Tunnel, which I will give a trial, if it is much cheaper. . . .

5 Dec. 1922

. . . Thanks for *Dethronements*, though I do not think it one of your good books, nothing like so good as *Angels and Ministers*. I do not believe that any of the people resembled or resemble your figures; and in the second dialogue the falsification of history is quite awful . . . To represent Chamberlain as an injured man, and Balfour as a man who injured him, is like saying that Christ crucified Pontius Pilate. 'The downfall of The Man of Business' (p. 6) was caused by eating, drinking, and smoking immoderately, and taking aperients instead of exercise. From the election of 1905 he came back in much better plight than Balfour, and was in a position to patronise him by finding him a seat. What Balfour did in his premiership was to prevent Chamberlain from quite ruining the party. Outside Parliament, Chamberlain was much the stronger of the two: everything in Unionism which was vulgar and sordid and greedy looked to him as its leader. When he started his precious tariff-reform, a thing which he had not intellect enough to comprehend, Balfour could not oppose him, especially as Free Trade was not the fetish to him that it is to Liberals: what he did was to temporise, and hold together, at the cost of much humiliation to himself and damage to his position, the party which Chamberlain would have torn asunder and led two thirds of it down a blind alley into

MEDALLION BY T. SPIELE SIMSON, 1922

a pit. His reward was to be driven from the leadership a few years later by those two thirds.

Page 64. The only occasion when Churchill came down to fight in the Central division of Birmingham was in 1885, before a Unionist party existed. In 1889, when Bright died, he did not come down, and the reason was Chamberlain, who was not going to have another cock crowing on his dunghill. On April 2, when the writ was moved, Hartington came to Churchill and said that Chamberlain was furious and in a state of extreme irritation. The question was decided straight away by a meeting of Chamberlain, Hartington, and Hicks Beach, Churchill having declared that he would accept their decision. That Balfour, who was then Chief Secretary for Ireland, had even an opportunity of hearing about it before it was settled is hardly possible. He was afterwards sent down to Birmingham to pacify the Conservatives there and persuade them to vote for Chamberlain's nominee; so I think your report of Chamberlain's remarks on the subject makes him out a very impudent dog.

Your affectionate brother (though I have received a press-cutting which authoritatively states that we are not brothers). . . .

18 Aug. 1925

. . . On the 27th I am going abroad for about a month, leaving behind me a nearly completed and in great part printed edition of Lucan with Basil Blackwell of Oxford. If the French kill me with one of these lethal railways of theirs, J. D. Duff of this college is to be asked to finish it and see it through the press. . . .

19 Sept. 1925

. . . The parody of me is the best I have seen, and indeed the only good one.

[This is the parody referred to: it was given me by its author, Hugh Kingsmill, in this form. Other versions have been published.

What, still alive at twenty two,
    A clean upstanding chap like you.
Sure, if your throat is hard to slit,
    Slit your girl's and swing for it.

Like enough, you won't be glad,
    When they come to hang you, lad.
But bacon's not the only thing
    That's cured by hanging from a string.

When the blotting-pad of night
    Sucks the latest drop of light,
Lads whose job is still to do
    Shall whet their knives and think of you.]

8 Dec. 1925

. . . An American named Keating wrote to me the other day and said he had bought a signed copy of *A Shropshire Lad* for £80. I suppose this is one of your commercial successes. . . .[1]

[1] See page 81.

29 Dec. 1925

. . . Thanks for your Christmas present.[1] I like *Blind Man's Buff* the best of the stories. *Farvingdon* I read when it came out, perhaps in Quilter's magazine.

At our last Feast I had the new Dean of Westminster next me, and he said he had long been wishing to thank me for the amusement he had derived from my writings, especially about Queen Victoria and her Ministers. So if I bring you money, you bring me fame.

Now that Hughley is burnt down it is curious to think that I never saw it; though it cannot have been much to see.

A happy new year to both of you. . . .

18 Nov. 1928

. . . Thanks for your book.[2] I think the best poem is *The Motion of Spring*, then perhaps *The Web of Night*. *Sunshade* is not particularly poetical, but very bright and ingenious; *The Cup of Memory* has a very good last line.

I was glad to hear from Kate that you are likely to be a candidate for super-tax. . . .

Trinity College
Cambridge
16 Feb. 1929

Only the archangel Raphael could recite my poetry properly, but I have no doubt you would do it quite nicely,

---

[1] *Odd Pairs.* [2] *The Love Concealed.*

and I shall not try to set up interfering wave-lengths.[1]
But understand that I incur no obligation to do the same
for you on your 70th birthday.

You had better select with care. The financial expert
who reorganised Grant Richards's business for his creditors
thought that he would like to read *A Shropshire Lad*.
He did, or as much as he could; then, in his own words,
'I put it behind the fire. Filthiest book I ever read: all
about . . .'[2]

> Now all day the horned herds
> Dance to the piping of the birds;
> Now the bumble-bee is rife,
> And other forms of insect life;
> The skylark in the sky so blue
> Now makes noise enough for two,
> And lovers on the grass so green
> – Muse, oh Muse, eschew th'obscene.

25 Feb. 1929

. . . I have no quarrel with your selection.[3] I shall not
attend your Sunday afternoon service. The Richards
Press are punctual and so far as I know honest in their
payments, and I am not so many hundred pounds to the
bad, in my capacity of author, as I once was. . . .

[1] On or about his 70th birthday, I gave a broadcast reading of his
poems.
[2] The rest is unprintable.
[3] For the broadcast.

Post card, undated, acknowledging a telegram sent on his 70th birthday

I received from you or C. a cheering exhortation[1] to shoulder the steg; and the Postmaster General reinforced it by repeating this word on the back of the telegram. I find that it means a male bird, especially a gander . . . I am in quest of one. April 1. . . .

12 May 1930

. . . No, I was not given the chance of being Laureate. I thought Masefield the right choice, as all the other good poets are too obviously unsuited for the official duties. . . .

1 March 1932

. . . Your generous offer[2] to pass on Coventry Patmore to me has its allurements, for I have often idly thought of writing an essay on him and have even been inclined sometimes to regard it, as you say, in the light of a duty, because nobody admires his best poetry enough, though the stupid papists may fancy they do. But it would give me more trouble than you can imagine, whereas I want peace in my declining years; and the result would not be good enough to yield me pride or even satisfaction. I should say as little as possible about his nasty mixture of piety and concupiscence; but his essay on English metre is the best thing ever written on the subject, though spoilt by one great mistake. . . .

---

[1] 'Shoulder the sky, my lad, and drink your ale.'
[2] An attempt to get him to write on Patmore for *Great Victorians*.

26 March 1932

. . . My knowledge of London restaurants is much out of date, and I can only have dined in two, both very expensive, in the last five years. I think you had better ask Grant Richards, unless you would like me to ask instead.

Thanks for your invitation, but I am shy of company, and in May there are many things which might interfere. Your approaching decease in January has attractions[1] . . .

28 Dec. 1932

. . . I am glad to have the report of your comparatively edifying end, which ought to go well on the stage; for I suppose by this time you are quite an accomplished actor. I observe that in order to make yourself more precious in the eyes of your redeemer you have blackened yourself with Basil's diabolism; and the exact phrase was 'I'm very fond of the devil'. The passage from *The Chinese Lantern* seems to me a judicious selection.

Love and a happy new year to both of you. . . .

25 Jan. 1933

. . . I have signed no end of copies[2] for the most un-deserving people, including a lot of my own students at University College, so I never make any difficulty about it. But your friend has come in for a slump in these fancy goods, I am afraid.[3]

[1] A play called *Nunc Dimittis*, also referred to in the two letters that follow.
[2] Of *A Shropshire Lad*.
[3] This refers to the price in the second-hand book-market for the original edition.

I saw from the papers that your death was attracting notice. I should like to hear you on the gramophone some day, but do not send me a record, which would be wasting it. . . .

20 May 1933

I am not proud of this,[1] which I wrote against my will, and am not sending copies outside the family. But its success here has taken me aback. The leader of our doctrinaire teachers of youth is reported to say that it will take more than twelve years to undo the harm I have done in an hour. . . .

Trinity College
Cambridge
24 May 1933

. . . The painful episode is closed;[2] but I may take this sentence from a paragraph which I cut out. 'Not only is it difficult to know the truth about anything, but to tell the truth when one knows it, to find words which will not obscure it or pervert it, is in my experience an exhausting effort.'

I did not say that poetry was the better for having no meaning, only that it can best be detected so.

I hear that Kipling says I am 'dead right' about the pit of the stomach.

I had better tell you before I forget it that the

---

[1] *The Name and Nature of Poetry.*
[2] The giving of the aforesaid lecture.

solicitor E. S. P. Haynes, who writes letters to the papers about the liberties of the subject, says in *A Lawyer's Notebook* that Belloc is the best living poet with the possible exception of you and me.

Your still affectionate brother, . . .

15 June 1933

. . . I should very much enjoy paying you the visit you propose, from Monday the 26th, say till Friday the 30th; but I suppose I ought to warn you that I am not in rude health. On the pretext that my heart was all over the place, after walking too much, I suppose, in the hot weather, the doctor sent me to bed for a week in a nursing home, where the heart must have disappointed him bitterly, for it behaved with the utmost decorum. The real bother is what I have often had before in the course of my life, depression and causeless anxiety. But I do not require attention, and am not a nuisance to Jeannie. . . .

14 Sept. 1933

. . . Many thanks for your *Victoria and Albert* which I shall read when I have got through things which are awaiting on my return. Your *Palace Plays* are always entertaining, however fabulous some of them may be.

My doctor inclines to think that my disagreeable tour in France has done me good, so I hope I shall soon find it out. . . .

30 Nov. 1933

. . . There was no enclosure in your letter, but I know what it was, and have already had an invitation from the people at University College, which, so far as I remember, I pretty explicitly declined. No doubt I should enjoy seeing you wrestle with the King of Terrors,[1] but though I am much better than I have been and no longer actually feeble, my spirits are rather low and the visit to London would worry me in prospect if not in act. . . .

6 Dec. 1933

Thanks for your Pre-Raphaelitism,[2] which I am glad to have, though some of the other contents of the volume seem pretty poor. What a wretched writer is Macan! and speller too.

I think that you make too much of Morris, and that the manner of *The Defence of Guenevere* is just one of his falsettos. He dropped it like a hot copper when he found it did not pay.

I should have liked to be told what to think of Burne-Jones. . . .'

[The next letter was in answer to my request to be allowed to include certain youthful poems in my reminiscences.]

[1] In *Nunc Dimittis*.
[2] A lecture, published with others, by the Royal Society of Literature.

15 June 1934

. . . I certainly am daunted by the prospect of staying at the ——¹ even in your company.

I should not mind the publication of the gnat and hat,² but the antimacassar, as I remember it, was not good enough. I remember nothing about 'Peter with small p'.

At least you are less premature with your reminiscences than most people now are. . . .

20 June 1934

. . . The more I think of the ——¹ the less I like it. That narrow street sees and hears the passage of more motors than almost any other in England, and the noise must begin early and cease late; and noise has been a trouble to me for the last twelvemonth.

I return the great poem corrected. *Peter piper* does not come up to my exalted notion of my genius, nor the stanza added to Cousin Agnes's poem.

Mr. Houston Martin is a lunatic, but not unintelligent. I have expressed so much contempt of his aims and activities that he has now let me alone for some time.

I do not know what is the poem of which he has the unique MS. . . .

29 Nov. 1934

. . . Many thanks for *Victoria Regina*: there are several pieces which I had not read before. What impresses

¹ An hotel, at which I had suggested our staying.
² 'At the door of my own little hovel.' (See p. 58).

me most is your cleverness in inventing detail. Perhaps Palmerston, as you think, is the best, though I think you take his side too much, and also make him too superior. There is a story by an eye-witness of his being reduced to tears by a jobation from the Prince Consort.

The verses come back to me,[1] but I feel as if I wrote 'stays' and not 'leaves', which may be an emendation of Clemence's prompted by her dislike for the harmless letter *s*. Also I don't use notes of admiration. . . .

9 June 1935

. . . Since the end of February I have grown much weaker, and more liable to shortness of breath and occasional thumping of the heart. The doctor does not want me to take walks of much more than a mile, and I myself am often inclined not to do much more than twice that amount. I still go up my 44 stairs two at a time, but that is in hopes of dropping dead at the top. As a tour in Yorkshire would be very pointless unless one could walk a fair amount, and up steeper gradients than those of Cambridgeshire, I no longer cherish the idea: otherwise it would have been very pleasant. I may be going to France in the autumn, but there I should be chiefly in towns.

I saw some notices, generally favourable, of your *Palace Plays* and am glad that the acting satisfied you and that there is a promising future for them in our revolted colonies. . . .

[1] 'Breathe, my lute, beneath my fingers.' (See p. 38).

15 June 1935

. . . Your idea of staying here with your car in the second week of August attracts me, as just now I am having very unpleasant nights and hardly feel courageous enough to contemplate a tour. You could of course have all your meals with me, but I could not with *certainty* offer you lodging for more than three consecutive nights, as we are not allowed to engage the Guest Room for more than three days at once. If nobody else wanted it, I could prolong the occupation a day at a time, but there would be the risk of interruption.

You have probably seen Ely and perhaps Peterborough, but there are a lot of good churches (of which I know only some) within reach of a car, and some quite nice country too. . . .

18 June 1935

. . . So far as I can see the dates you propose would suit me equally; but I have been sent here[1] 'for a fortnight or perhaps a week' by reason of Cheyne-Stokes breathing, described in Arnold Bennett's *Clayhanger* where it is an embellishment of the death-bed of the hero's father. They are getting the better of it with morphia, and I slept last night.

If I were in proper health I should at this moment be representing Cambridge at the tercentenary of the French Academy. . . .

---

[1] The Evelyn Nursing Home, Cambridge.

28 Oct. 1935

. . . Thanks for your offer to help with my books, but I do not think it is a task on which I ought to employ your energies, nor on which you would find very much to do. The boys of the college Library seem to be experienced in such matters, and Gow is very kindly giving an eye to the matter. He told me that you were coming here next month and suggested that I might wish to consult you about discarding or retaining books, but I do not think this will prove much of a problem. Probably nothing which I am discarding is anything which you would wish to take. The main difficulty is to find space in the new rooms.

I shall be here[1] probably at least ten days more, and at this moment I am reduced to great weakness by sleepless and distressed nights, the sedatives having failed; so that even if I were back in College I could not offer you hospitality or society. None the less I am grateful to you for offering to sacrifice so much of your time. . . .

8 Nov. 1935

. . . I should be glad to see you between 5 o'clock and 6.30, on Monday and at the earlier hour, if you let me know, I could offer you tea. I shall not be leaving before that day.

I am much more tranquil, and the dropsy has almost disappeared, so the doctor is quite satisfied, but he does not realise how weak I am. . . .

[1] The Evelyn Nursing Home, Cambridge.

10 Jan. 1925[1]

. . . Days fly and I am little better at conducting business, so I shall be grateful if you will take it upon you to say that I am not prepared to give permission about *Hell Gate*.[2] I am not conscious of any strong objection, and perhaps I am foolish, but I am not strong enough to decide affirmatively. . . .

11 March 1936

. . . I rejoice that you have made a fortune. Do not squander it as you did the proceeds of *The Englishwoman*.

When you wrote to me about the setting of *Hell Gate* I was very ill and could not make up my mind to say yes; but I now do not mind consenting. The orchestra will *drown* the words, which must be pretty bad if a composer had an overwhelming admiration for them.

> Brightness falls from the air;
> Queens have died young and fair;
> Dust hath closed Helen's eye.

T. Nashe
In time of plague

[This is the last letter I had from him. The quotation is in answer to my request to be told who wrote it.]

---

[1] Actually 1936.
[2] For the setting of it to music.

Letters to Mr. Houston Martin, a young graduate of Pennsyl-
vania endowed in full measure with the American gift of
refusing to take No. These letters usually began 'Dear Mr.
Martin', and were signed 'Yours sincerely, A. E. Housman'.

25 Nov. 1932

. . . I am obliged and flattered by your letter, but it is
now a great many years since I began to refuse requests
for poems written out in my own hand, and therefore
you must not mind if you receive the same answer as
many others. . . .

28 March 1933

. . . It was kind of you to write to me on my birthday.
You are right in supposing that I do not look with favour
on the collecting of first editions and autographs,
but it is a vice which is sometimes found in otherwise
virtuous persons, of whom you doubtless are one.

It is many years since I have had a photograph taken,
but I have found and enclose an old one, taken about the
time when I was writing *A Shropshire Lad*.

I could not say that I have a favourite among my
poems. Thomas Hardy's was No. XXVII in *A Shropshire
Lad*,[1] and I think it may be the best, though it is not
the most perfect. . . .

(*Accompanying a manuscript copy of 'Loveliest of trees'*)

20 Nov. 1933

. . . Apparently you have been searching the Scriptures
and have lighted on the 18th chapter of St. Luke. I am

---

[1] 'Is my team ploughing.'

ashamed of myself for showing no more firmness of mind than the unjust judge, but such infatuation as yours is quite intimidating. I observe that your photograph wears a grin of assured success.

I gave the manuscript of *A Shropshire Lad* to the library of this college, and that of *Last Poems* to the Fitzwilliam Museum in Cambridge.

I was not born in Shropshire at all, but near the town of Bromsgrove in Worcestershire. The Shropshire hills were our western horizon, and hence my sentiment for the county, I suppose. . . .

14 Dec. 1933

. . . You are an engaging madman and write more agreeably than many sane persons; but if I write anything of an autobiographical nature, as I have sometimes idly thought of doing, I shall send it to the British Museum to be kept under lock and key for 50 years. There is no biography of Matthew Arnold (whom I am glad to see that you read) in accordance with his own advice; so there certainly need be none of me.

Your last enquiry, though frivolous, is harmless, and I may reply that I never do sign my name in full except in documents where I am directed to do so. . . .

23 March 1934

. . . You are always kind and friendly and your anthology of opinions[1] ought to foster my self-esteem and smooth my descent to the grave.

[1] A collection of opinions on A.E.H.'s poems, extracted by Mr. Houston Martin from a number of American authors.

I translated three lyrics from Aeschylus, Sophocles, and Euripides, respectively, in A. W. Pollard's *Odes from the Greek Dramatists* (Stott, 1890). The parody called *Fragment of a Greek Tragedy* was first printed in 1884 in the School Magazine of Bromsgrove: they still have half-a-dozen copies, which on my advice they are not selling till I am dead, when you may be able to get one for your great collection. But it has often been reprinted, as in the *Cornhill Magazine* for 1901 (I think), and the *Yale Review* for Jan. 1928. . . .

14 April 1934

. . . I have never seen the misprint 'tramping' [for 'trampling'] in no. VII of *A Shropshire Lad*. Perhaps you have come across it in some of the pirated American editions. Even in the authorised edition by Holt there are disgraceful misprints. . . .

The stanza prefixed to no. L of *A Shropshire Lad* is traditional. One version is "drunkenest".

At Buildwas there is the ruin of an abbey church, not large but fairly complete, of Norman date.

I am Worcestershire by birth: Shropshire was our western horizon, which made me feel romantic about it. I do not know the county well, except in parts, and some of my topographical details are wrong and imaginary. The Wrekin is wooded, and Wenlock Edge along the western side, but the Clees and most of the other hills are grass or heather. In the southern half of the county, to which I have confined myself, the hills are generally long ridges running from north to south, with valleys, broad or narrow, between. The northern half is part of the great Cheshire plain. The Wrekin is isolated. . . .

You will not expect me to approve your project. I am appalled to hear of your copying my articles in the *Classical Quarterly.* . . .

26 Sept. 1934

. . . You ought to have known better than to send me the copy of *A Shropshire Lad.* American publishers have a perfect right to issue unauthorised copies, but for me to sign them would be an indignity or an excess of magnanimity. I am also deaf to fantastic requests that I should write my name in full or add special stuff for you. One thing I am prepared to do, which might gratify your depraved mind: if you like to send me *New Year's Eve* I can make and initial a correction which I was too late to make before it was printed. If I possess a copy of *Parta Quies,*[1] which I do not know to be the case, I do not know where to find it. *A Shropshire Lad* and *New Poems* [sic] will never be joined together while I am here to prevent it, and I think it a silly notion.

I congratulate you on your 20th birthday and your approach, I hope, to years of discretion. I did not realise how frightfully young you were: it explains and perhaps excuses much.

[1] Originally published in *Waifs and Strays*, an Oxford magazine. Afterwards included in *More Poems* as *Alta Quies*.

I thank you for your good wishes and you have mine. . . .

17 Oct. 1934

. . . I have had to make more than one correction in the copy of *New Year's Eve* which I return.

'*New Poems*' was only a slip of my senile pen.

Fragment composed in a dream I do not know,[1] or have forgotten. I suppose it would be impossible for me to explain to you, perhaps to any American, the impropriety of your conduct in writing, as you seem to have done, to ask famous writers their opinion of me. I hope that some of them, at any rate, have ignored your letters.

Bredon Hill is in Worcestershire on the edge of Gloucestershire. That poem was written early, before I knew the book would be a Shropshire book. Abdon Burf is the highest part of the Brown Clee, which is the highest hill in Shropshire, but will soon cease to be so, as they are quarrying the top away. . . .

27 Sept. 1935

. . . Your questions, though frivolous, are not indecent, so I suppose I must humour you.

I do not admire the oracle poem[2] quite so much as some people do. The italics, as elsewhere, are equivalent to inverted commas, and give the supposed words of the oracle.

---

[1] This is in fact the quotation beginning 'When the bells', printed on p. 220. It was privately (and quite unofficially) printed in 1931 in an edition of 37 copies.

[2] ' 'Tis mute, the word they went to hear,'

Alterations were made by the printer in the 2nd edition of *A Shropshire Lad*. The proofs were not sent to me for correction.

I certainly shall not issue my preface to Manilius separately. The Introductory Lecture of 1892 was reprinted in 1933 by two young men named John Carter and John Sparrow in an edition of 100 copies, not for sale. I shall not reprint it.

Hardy and I never talked about my poems. I think it was Mrs. Hardy who told me his opinion.

Certainly I have never regretted the publication of my poems. The reputation which they brought me, though it gives me no lively pleasure, is something like a mattress interposed between me and the hard ground. The lectures I care very little about.

With all good wishes for your health and sanity. . . .

22 March 1936

. . . I was very ill at the beginning of the year, and I am now again in a nursing home. I hope that if you can restrain your indecent ardour for a little I shall be properly dead and your proposed work will not be by its nature unbecoming. But the hope is not more than a hope, for my family are tough and long-lived, unless they take to drink.

Do not send me your manuscript. Worse than the practice of writing books about living men is the conduct of living men in supervising such books. I do not forbid you to quote extracts from my letters.

Letters to Mr. Seymour Adelman, an American scholar and bibliophile, also an ardent collector of A.E.H.'s books and manuscripts. The letters begin 'Dear Mr. Adelman' are signed 'Yours sincerely, A. E. Housman'. The explanatory notes accompanying these letters have been kindly supplied to me by Mr. Adelman.

(Note: In the Spring of 1928, the Literary Society of my art-school asked me to speak on the poems. In preparing my talk, I encountered various conjectures which Professor Housman alone could answer.)

6 May 1928

. . . The words of mine which have reached your ears may be something like this. I can no more define poetry than a terrier can define a rat; but he knows a rat when he comes across one, and I recognise poetry by definite physical sensations, either down the spine, or at the back of the throat, or in the pit of the stomach.

The influence of Heine is evident in *A Shropshire Lad*. For Keats I have the greatest admiration, but I should not have thought that my writing had any affinity to his.

An illustrated edition was produced to please the publisher: the illustrations were Shropshire landscapes by William Hyde. They were in colour, which always looks vulgar, and the edition is now withdrawn. The late Lovat Fraser made drawings which he called illustrations, and I suppose that they had artistic merit, but illustrations they were not. All the figures, when there were figures, were put into eighteenth-century costume, and No. XXX was represented by a fat old man asleep on a chair. . . .

Neither illustrators nor composers care twopence about words, and generally do not understand them.

(Note: Sometime in 1928 I bought a first edition of *A Shropshire Lad*. It had formerly belonged to Mr. Reginald Turner, one of Oscar Wilde's most steadfast friends. Because of this association, and knowing how deeply *The Ballad of Reading Gaol* was indebted to your brother's poems, I tried to find out all I could that linked Wilde and *A Shropshire Lad*.)

21 June 1928

. . . *A Shropshire Lad* was published while Mr. Wilde was in prison, and when he came out I sent him a copy myself. Robert Ross told me that when he visited his friend in jail he learnt some of the poems by heart and recited them to him; so that was his first acquaintance with them. I do not think I ever heard of Reginald Turner. Parts of *The Ballad of Reading Gaol* are above Wilde's average, but I suspect they were written by Lord Alfred Douglas[1]. . . .

(Note: On February 14, 1929, there was purchased

---

[1] For Lord Alfred Douglas's version of the matter, see his *Autobiography* (1929), pp. 157-8.

for my order at Sotheby's, London, an autograph manuscript of your brother's delightfully malicious *Fragment
of a Greek Tragedy*. On receiving the manuscript,
I inquired of Professor Housman as to its various published appearances, and whether I might print it in
facsimile for private distribution.)

16 March 1929

. . . The *Fragment of a Greek Tragedy* was first
published in 1884 in *The Bromsgrovian*, a school
magazine, and has been reprinted in three or four
places, the last of which, I think, was 'at the Snail's
Pace Press', Amherst, in 1925. They have at Bromsgrove School about half-a-dozen copies of the original
issue, but I have advised them not to sell them till after
my death.

Your amiable desire to print a limited edition in
facsimile is one which I should do everything in my
power to thwart. And I am very much puzzled about
the autograph. I did not know that any existed, and I
told the vendor so. You may be able to judge by com-
paring the handwriting with this letter. If the paper is
stamped with 'K. E. S. Bromsgrove', it cannot be
mine. . . .

(Note: I was not particularly surprised to find Professor
Housman questioning the authenticity of the *Fragment*
manuscript. To settle all doubt, I made photographs of
the manuscript's five pages and sent them to Cambridge.)

7 April 1929

. . . The supposed autograph is not mine. It is a copy, not quite accurate, from *The Bromsgrovian*; and the date is wrong.

To prevent you from bringing an action against the innocent though credulous lady who has got your money, I have written out the *Fragment* in the form to which it has been brought by successive republications. I shall be obliged if, in return, you will send me your worthless purchase. . . .

28 April 1929

Thanks for sending me the *Fragment*, which I have put in the fire, though I don't think it was meant for a forgery.

I must have written the fragment three or four times for the various magazines in which it was printed, but I do not know that any of the MSS survive.

The people at Bromsgrove might possibly sell you a copy of *The Bromsgrovian* if you offered a sufficiently absurd price; but I cannot encourage or countenance such proceedings. . . .

30 Dec. 1933

. . . The paragraph in the catalogue,[1] as you surmise, contains a great deal of error. It was only one publisher who was offered *A Shropshire Lad* and declined it. The firm which published it at my expense was the joint

---

[1] An American book-catalogue, stating that A.E.H. tried every known publisher for his verse and that they all turned it down.

A. E. HOUSMAN
(Passport Photograph)
AGED 70

firm of Kegan Paul, Trench, Trübner & Co., which had published a good deal of belles lettres. The number of copies printed was 500, and the time it took to sell them (at 2/6 each) was rather more than two years. There was no contract about republishing: I kept Mr. Grant Richards waiting until Kegan Paul & Co. signified that a 2nd edition would have to be printed again at my own expense. It is a great exaggeration to talk of a boom in connexion with the 2nd edition: such boom as there was began with the war of 1914. . . .

From letters to Mrs. Ralph Thicknesse, a friend whose suffrage sympathies he did not share. Her husband wrote a brochure entitled 'The Rights and Wrongs of Women'. All the letters began 'Dear Mrs. Thicknesse', and were signed 'Yours sincerely, A. E. Housman'.

11 June 1900

. . . I am sorry to hear Ray has been so ill, and I hope he continues to improve. I trust it was not the emotion of my farewell interview which gave a bad turn to his illness.

I ordered the *Londoner* some days ago, but W. H. Smith and Sons have not yet sent it: I don't know whether this is pure negligence on their part, or whether they have detected in it anything which they think would be likely to demoralise me.

On Saturday Karl Pearson and I are going for a walk in Buckinghamshire, to find a farmer who lays a par-

ticular kind of eggs, which tend to prove that there is
no God. . . .

11 Aug. 1909

. . . My blood boils. This is not due to the recent
commencement of summer, but to the Wrongs of
Woman, with which I have been making myself
acquainted. 'She cannot serve on any Jury'; and yet
she bravely lives on. 'She cannot serve in the army or
navy' – oh cruel, cruel! – 'except' – this adds insult to
injury – 'as a nurse'. They do not even employ a
Running Woman instead of a Running Man for prac-
tising marksmanship. I have been making marginal
additions. 'She cannot be ordained a Priest or Deacon':
add *nor become a Freemason*. 'She cannot be a member
of the Royal Society': add *nor of the Amateur Boxing
Association*. In short, your unhappy sex seem to have
nothing to look forward to, excepting contracting a valid
marriage as soon as they are 12 years old; and that must
soon pall.

Thanks for the picture card. I did not know, or had
forgotten, that you were at Woodbridge. If you can find
an old hat of Edward FitzGerald's they will let you write
three columns about it in the *Athenaeum*. But some
literary people are so proud that they despise these
avenues to fame. . . .

8 March 1913

. . . The chief excitements of the term here have been
an agitation, by a highly undistinguished set of persons,

to introduce conscription for undergraduates, as a last effort to frighten the Germans; and an exhibition of post-impressionist undergraduate art, which is calculated to frighten the Germans a good deal more.

My respects to both of you. . . .

24 Nov. 1914

. . . The thirst for blood is raging among the youth of England. More than half the undergraduates are away, but mostly not at the front, because they all want to be officers. I am going out when they make me a Field Marshal. Meanwhile I have three nephews being inoculated for typhoid and catching pneumonia on Salisbury Plain and performing other acts of war calculated to make the German Emperor realise that he is a very misguided man. . . .

7 March 1915

. . . On the 16th I shall be beyond the Channel or beneath it: more probably the former, for steamers seem to ram submarines better than submarines torpedo steamers. Hitherto I have always refused to go to the Riviera, but now is my chance, when the worst classes who infest it are away.

. . . Here we have 1000 undergraduates and 20,000 soldiers, 500 of them billeted in the building in which I write these lines, and one of them doing a quick-step overhead. . . .

10 March 1924

. . . Last year a French school-ma'm wrote to me wanting to translate *A Shropshire Lad* and asking what share of the proceeds I should expect. I replied that I should take nothing; but then mine is a character of unusual and almost disagreeable nobility. . . .

Letter to the Countess Cave in reply to her request to be allowed to reprint in her book of Ants, some verses which had appeared anonymously in 'The Bromsgrovian'.

7 Feb. 1933

Dear Lady Cave,

I have no reason to think that the anonymous author of the verses you mention, if still living, would have any objection to your using them, and I myself, to whom they should not be attributed, have none; but I suppose that the copyright, if there is any, belongs to the editor and editorial committee of *The Bromsgrovian*. . .

I am yours sincerely

A. E. Housman.

To a further letter on the same subject he replied:

31 Oct. 1933

Dear Lady Cave,

Many thanks for your letter. I am pleased to hear of your discretion in preserving the anonymity of the poem, and I do not grudge Lord Darling any credit or discredit which may wrongly attach itself to him. . . .

*To Professor Arthur Platt, an old friend and colleague
at University College, London.*

6 April 1916

Dear Platt,

If you prefer Aeschylus to Manilius you are no true
scholar; you must be deeply tainted with literature, as
indeed I always suspected that you were.

The Bible is supposed to be full of types, and perhaps
St Paul – ce type là – prefigures Don Quixote. The
resemblances you mention had not struck me, but they
will bear thinking on. I wonder if St Paul's experiences
in the third heaven are susceptible of the same explanation as Don Quixote's in the moon.

Yours sincerely,

A. E. Housman.

*To a correspondent who asked him to tell her the order
in which he wrote the stanzas of the poem he refers to in
'The Name and Nature of Poetry'*

12 April 1935

. . . I have received several guesses at the order of some
or all of the stanzas, but I do not let the truth be known,
because then everyone would begin to pretend that it
was obvious to them. If I had to guess myself, I am sure
I could not tell which was last and which last but one;
though I think I could guess which two came first. . . .

POEMS

o

POEMS

NOTE ON THE ADDITIONAL POEMS

TEN or twelve years ago I was told by A.E.H. that he was leaving it for me to decide what of his remaining verse was to be published after his death; and for my guidance he then said he wished me to include nothing which I considered inferior to anything that had already appeared.

I did not then admit to him that the inclusion in *A Shropshire Lad* of a poem which I thought inferior to the rest would make my task easier than it might otherwise have been, nor am I now going to say which that poem was. But I have, to the best of my judgment, included nothing in the two selections for which I am responsible – *More Poems* and those which here follow – of a lower standard than that which he indicated. But since I am now publishing a second selection, it may be well for me to explain why I am doing so. My anxiety not to leave out anything that might reasonably be regarded as sufficiently complete and up to standard was naturally very great; but I was equally anxious not to include in my selection too many poems of a border-line character, or of a brevity which might have the effect of making the whole appear somewhat fragmentary. But as the three books of published poems may now be regarded as constituting the canon of my brother's poetry, I feel myself freer to make these few additions, and in what I have now to say about them I give reasons why my second thoughts have resulted in their publication.

With regard to the poems which are of one verse only, I have already stated why they were not included in *More Poems*. *Atys* was one of the two poems which A.E.H. sent for me to choose from when I was editing *The Venture* in 1903: but he kept no fair copy of it; and when I asked him why he had not included it in *Last Poems* he said because it was written in a metre he was so fond of, that he always doubted the merit of any poem in which he had succumbed to its attraction. The fact that he only left a very rough draft, difficult to reconstruct, and nearly impossible had I not remembered the poem fairly well, showed that he had definitely abandoned it.

The poem here included in which I have most interest,. and am most glad to have preserved, 'Ask me no more for fear I should reply', was, I feel sure, put aside by A.E.H. because he had used a refrain made familiar in one of Tennyson's lyrics in *The Princess*; and I kept it out of *More Poems* for the same reason; adverse critics would have fastened on this for belittlement of its beauty – a risk I did not care to run in the first instance, but which I am prepared to face now.

Several of the other poems were omitted from *More Poems* because a majority of those I consulted were mildly against them; in some instances I was so myself.

The device used in 'Oh is it the jar of Nations', of question and answer between living and dead, was employed with much better effect in the far finer poem, 'Is my team ploughing'. But apart from that comparison the poem has this right to preservation – that it is up to standard.

In other cases, when conflict of opinion has been even, and my conscience left me free, I have decided for present inclusion of what was before rejected.

About the last poem (XVIII) I feel quite sure that though it is not of a high standard it says something which A.E.H. very much wished to say, but perhaps preferred not to say in his own lifetime. For literary reasons I omitted it from *More Poems*; for the reason already stated in the memoir I give it here.

I

ATYS

'Lydians, lords of Hermus river,
   Sifters of the golden loam,
See you yet the lances quiver
   And the hunt returning home?'

'King, the star that shuts the even
   Calls the sheep from Tmolus down;
Home return the doves from heaven,
   And the prince to Sardis town.'

From the hunting heavy laden
   Up the Mysian road they ride;
And the star that mates the maiden
   Leads his son to Croesus' side.

'Lydians, under stream and fountain
   Finders of the golden vein,
Riding from Olympus mountain,
   Lydians, see you Atys plain?'

'King, I see the Phrygian stranger
   And the guards in hunter's trim,
Saviours of thy son from danger;
   Them I see. I see not him.'

'Lydians, as the troop advances,
   – It is eve and I am old –
Tell me why they trail their lances,
   Washers of the sands of gold.

'I am old and day is ending
   And the wildering night comes on;
Up the Mysian entry wending,
   Lydians, Lydians, what is yon?'

Hounds behind their master whining,
   Huntsmen pacing dumb beside,
On his breast the boar-spear shining,
   Home they bear his father's pride.

II

Oh were he and I together,
  Shipmates on the fleeted main,
Sailing through the summer weather
  To the spoil of France or Spain.

Oh were he and I together,
  Locking hands and taking leave,
Low upon the trampled heather
  In the battle lost at eve.

Now are he and I asunder
  And asunder to remain;
Kingdoms are for others' plunder,
  And content for other slain.

I I I

When Adam walked in Eden young,
　　Happy, 'tis writ, was he,
While high the fruit of knowledge hung
　　Unbitten on the tree.

Happy was he the livelong day;
　　I doubt 'tis written wrong:
The heart of man, for all they say,
　　Was never happy long.

And now my feet are tired of rest,
　　And here they will not stay,
And the soul fevers in my breast
　　And aches to be away.

IV

It is no gift I tender,
  A loan is all I can;
But do not scorn the lender;
  Man gets no more from man.

Oh, mortal man may borrow
  What mortal man can lend;
And 'twill not end tomorrow,
  Though sure enough 'twill end.

If death and time are stronger,
  A love may yet be strong;
The world will last for longer,
  But this will last for long.

V

Here are the skies, the planets seven,
And all the starry train;
Content you with the mimic heaven,
And on the earth remain.[1]

Written by A.E.H. on the flyleaf of a copy of *Manilius*, Book I, which he
gave to Walter Headlam.

V I

Ask me no more, for fear I should reply;
  Others have held their tongues, and so can I,
Hundreds have died, and told no tale before:
  Ask me no more, for fear I should reply –

How one was true and one was clean of stain
  And one was braver than the heavens are high,
And one was fond of me:[1] and all are slain.
  Ask me no more, for fear I should reply.

V I I

He would not stay for me; and who can wonder?
  He would not stay for me to stand and gaze.
I shook his hand and tore my heart in sunder
  And went with half my life about my ways.

Alternative reading: 'kind to me'.

V I·I I

Now to her lap the incestuous earth
  The son she bore has ta'en.
And other sons she brings to birth
  But not my friend again.

I X

When the bells justle in the tower
  The hollow night amid,
Then on my tongue the taste is sour[1]
  Of all I ever did.

X

Oh, on my breast in days hereafter
  Light the earth should lie,
Such weight to bear is now the air,
  So heavy hangs the sky.

[1] Alternative reading: 'Then to my heart the thought is sour'.

XI

GOD'S ACRE

Morning up the eastern stair
Marches, azuring the air,
And the foot of twilight still
Is stolen toward the western sill.
Blithe the maids to milking, blithe
Men in hayfields stone the scythe;
All the land's alive around
Except the churchyard's idle ground.
There's empty acres west and east,
But 'tis from God's we gather least,
This hopeless garden that they sow
With the seeds that never grow.
They shall have breath that never were,
But he that was shall have it ne'er;
The unconceived and unbegot
Shall look on heaven, but he shall not.
The heart with many wild-fires lit,
Ice is not so cold as it.
The thirst that rivers could not lay
A little dust has quenched for aye;
And in a fathom's compass lie
Thoughts much wider than the sky.

XII

AN EPITAPH

Stay, if you list, O passer by the way;
Yet night approaches; better not to stay.
 I never sigh, nor flush, nor knit the brow,
 Nor grieve to think how ill God made me, now.
Here, with one balm for many fevers found,
Whole of an ancient evil, I sleep sound.

XIII

Oh turn not in from marching
 To taverns on the way.
The drought and thirst and parching
 A little dust will lay,
 And take desire away.

Oh waste no words a-wooing
 The soft sleep to your bed;
She is not worth pursuing,
 You will so soon be dead;
 And death will serve instead.

XIV

'Oh is it the jar of nations,
  The noise of a world run mad,
The fleeing of earth's foundations?'
  Yes, yes, lie quiet, my lad.

'Oh is it my country calling?
  And who will my country find
To shore up the sky from falling?'
  My business; never you mind.

'Oh is it the newsboys crying
  Lost battle, retreat, despair,
And honour and England dying?'
  Well, fighting-cock, what if it were?

The devil this side of the darnels
  Is having a dance with man,
And quarrelsome chaps in charnels
  Must bear it as best they can.

XV

'Tis five years since, 'An end,' said I;
'I'll march no further, time to die.
All's lost; no more has heaven to give.'
Worse it has given, and yet I live.

I shall not die to-day, no fear;
I shall live yet for many a year,
And see worse ills and worse again,
And die of age and not of pain.

When God would rear from earth aloof
The blue height of the hollow roof,
He sought him pillars sure and strong,
And ere he found them sought them long.

The stark steel splintered from the thrust,
The basalt mountain sprang to dust,
The blazing pier of diamond flawed
In shards of rainbows all abroad.

What found he, that the heavens stand fast?
What pillar proven fine at last
Bears up so light that world-seen span?
The heart of man, the heart of man.

XVI

Some can gaze and not be sick,
But I could never learn the trick.
There's this to say for blood and breath,
They give a man a taste for death.

XVII

The stars have not dealt me the worst they could do:
My pleasures are plenty, my troubles are two.
But oh, my two troubles they reave me of rest,
The brains in my head and the heart in my breast.

O grant me the ease that is granted so free,
The birthright of multitudes, give it to me,
That relish their victuals and rest on their bed
With flint in the bosom and guts in the head.

XVIII

Oh who is that young sinner with the handcuffs on his
wrists?
And what has he been after that they groan and shake
their fists?
And wherefore is he wearing such a conscience-stricken air?
Oh they're taking him to prison for the colour of his hair.

'Tis a shame to human nature, such a head of hair as his;
In the good old time 'twas hanging for the colour that it is;
Though hanging isn't bad enough and flaying would be fair
For the nameless and abominable colour of his hair.

Oh a deal of pains he's taken and a pretty price he's paid
To hide his poll or dye it of a mentionable shade;
But they've pulled the beggar's hat off for the world
to see and stare,
And they're taking him to justice for the colour of his hair.

Now 'tis oakum for his fingers and the treadmill for his
feet,
And the quarry-gang on Portland in the cold and in the
heat,
And between his spells of labour in the time he has to
spare
He can curse the God that made him for the colour of
his hair.

LIGHT VERSE AND PARODIES

LIGHT VERSE AND PARODIES

NOTE

These rhymes and parodies were written at various dates between 1880 and 1927. Nos. I and II are the earliest. The *Fragment of an English Opera* was sent to assist me when I was writing a libretto in 1907.

The *Fragment of a Didactic Poem on Latin Grammar* was included in a paper on Erasmus Darwin, given by A.E.H. to the Students of University College, London. In the author's words, it was 'intended to convey to the reader, in language at once appropriate to the subject and intrinsically beautiful, the information that adjectives agree with their substantives in gender, number and case'.

I

The shades of night were falling fast,
  And the rain was falling faster,
When through an Alpine village passed
  An Alpine village pastor:
A youth who bore mid snow and ice
  A bird that wouldn't chirrup,
And a banner with the strange device --
  'Mrs. Winslow's soothing syrup'.

'Beware the pass', the old man said,
  'My bold, my desperate fellah;
Dark lowers the tempest overhead,
  And you'll want your umberella;
And the roaring torrent is deep and wide --
  You may hear how loud it washes.'
But still that clarion voice replied:
  'I've got my old goloshes.'

'Oh, stay', the maiden said, 'and rest
  (For the wind blows from the nor'ward)
Thy weary head upon my breast --
  And please don't think I'm forward.'
A tear stood in his bright blue eye,
  And he gladly would have tarried;
But still he answered with a sigh:
  'Unhappily I'm married.'

II

As I was walking slowly
　　Among the grassy hay,
Oh, there I met an old man
　　Whose nerves had given way:
His heels were in an ants' nest,
　　His head was in a tree,
And his arms went round and round and round,
　　And he squealed repeatedly.

I waited very kindly,
　　And attended to his wants;
For I put his heels into the tree,
　　And his head among the ants:
I tied his hands with a boot-lace,
　　And I filled his mouth with hay,
And I said 'Good-bye; fine morning:
　　Many happy returns of the day!'

He could not squeal distinctly,
　　And his arms would not go round;
Yet he did not leave off making
　　A discontented sound.
I gazed at him a little while,
　　As I walked among the trees,
And I said 'When old men's nerves give way,
　　How hard they are to please!'

231

III

As into the garden Elizabeth ran
Pursued by the just indignation of Ann,
She trod on an object that lay in her road,
She trod on an object that looked like a toad.

It looked like a toad, and it looked so because
A toad was the actual object it was;
And after supporting Elizabeth's tread
It looked like a toad that was visibly dead.

Elizabeth, leaving her footprint behind,
Continued her flight on the wings of the wind,
And Ann in her anger was heard to arrive
At the toad that was not any longer alive.

She was heard to arrive, for the firmament rang
With the sound of a scream and the noise of a bang,
As her breath on the breezes she broadly bestowed
And fainted away on Elizabeth's toad.

Elizabeth, saved by the sole of her boot,
Escaped her insensible sister's pursuit;
And if ever hereafter she irritates Ann,
She will tread on a toad if she possibly can.

IV

'In the back back garden, Thomasina
  Did you recently vociferate a squeal?'
'Oh, I trod upon an amphisbaena,
    And it bit me on the toe and on the heel.
      Yes, it bit me (do you know)
      With its tail upon the toe,
  While it bit me with its head upon the heel!'

'How excessively distracting and confusing.
    Pray what, Thomasina, did you do?'
'Oh, I took the garden scissors I was using
    And I snipped it irretrievably in two.
      And it split with such a scrunch
      That I shall not want my lunch.
  And if you had heard the noise no more would you.'

'And where, Thomasina, are the sections
    Of the foe that you courageously repressed?'
'Oh, they ran away in opposite directions,
    And they vanished in the east and in the west.
      And the way they made me squint,
      It would melt a heart of flint,
  And I think that I will go upstairs and rest.'

V

Away with bloodshed, I love not such,
But Jane Eliza snores too much.

I bought a serpent that bites and stings
For three-and-sixpence or four shillings.

When Jane Eliza began to snore
I put it under her bedroom door.

The serpent had neither bit nor stung,
It had only just put out its tongue,

When Jane Eliza fell out of bed
And bumped upon it and killed it dead.

It showed off none of its pretty tricks
That cost four shillings or three-and-six;

It had no time to sting or bite
Nor even to utter the words 'Good night'.

So three-and-sixpence at least is gone,
And Jane Eliza, she still snores on.

VI

Amelia mixed the mustard,
  She mixed it good and thick;
She put it in the custard
  And made her Mother sick,
And showing satisfaction
  By many a loud huzza
'Observe' said she 'the action
  Of mustard on Mamma.'

VII

THE ELEPHANT, OR THE FORCE OF HABIT

A tail behind, a trunk in front,
Complete the usual elephant.
The tail in front, the trunk behind,
Is what you very seldom find.

If you for specimens should hunt
With trunks behind and tails in front,
That hunt would occupy you long;
The force of habit is so strong.

VIII

INFANT INNOCENCE

Reader, behold! this monster wild
Has gobbled up the infant child.
The infant child is not aware
It has been eaten by the bear.

[This was accompanied by a picture of a large fat
bear, a nursemaid fleeing in the distance, and an empty
perambulator.]

236

IX

O have you caught the tiger?
   And can you hold him tight?
And what immortal hand or eye
Could frame his fearful symmetry?
   And does he try to bite?

Yes, I have caught the tiger,
   And he was hard to catch.
O tiger, tiger, do not try
To put your tail into my eye,
   And do not bite and scratch.

Yes, I have caught the tiger.
   O tiger, do not bray!
And what immortal hand or eye
Could frame his fearful symmetry.
   I should not like to say.

And may I see the tiger?
   I should indeed delight
To see so large an animal
Without a voyage to Bengal.
   And mind you hold him tight.

Yes, you may see the tiger;
   It will amuse you much.
The tiger is, as you will find,
A creature of the feline kind.
   And mind you do not touch.

And do you feed the tiger,
　And do you keep him clean?
He has a less contented look
Than in the Natural History book,
　And seems a trifle lean.

Oh yes, I feed the tiger,
　And soon he will be plump;
I give him groundsel fresh and sweet,
And much canary-seed to eat,
　And wash him at the pump.

It seems to me the tiger
　Has not been lately fed,
Not for a day or two at least;
And that is why the noble beast
　Has bitten off your head.

X

INHUMAN HENRY
or
CRUELTY TO FABULOUS ANIMALS

Oh would you know why Henry sleeps,
And why his mourning Mother weeps,
And why his weeping Mother mourns?
He was unkind to unicorns.

No unicorn, with Henry's leave,
Could dance upon the lawn at eve,
Or gore the gardener's boy in spring
Or do the very slightest thing.

No unicorn could safely roar,
And dash its nose against the door,
Nor sit in peace upon the mat
To eat the dog, or drink the cat.

Henry would never in the least
Encourage the heraldic beast:
If there were unicorns about
He went and let the lion out.

The lion, leaping from its chain
And glaring through its tangled mane,
Would stand on end and bark and bound
And bite what unicorns it found.

239

And when the lion bit a lot
Was Henry sorry? He was not.
What did his jumps betoken? Joy.
He was a bloody-minded boy.

The Unicorn is not a Goose,
And when they saw the lion loose
They grew increasingly aware
That they had better not be there.

And oh, the unicorn is fleet
And spurns the earth with all its feet.
The lion had to snap and snatch
At tips of tails it could not catch.

Returning home in temper bad,
It met the sanguinary lad,
And clasping Henry with its claws
It took his legs between its jaws.

'Down, lion, down!' said Henry, 'cease!
My legs immediately release.'
His formidable feline pet
Made no reply, but only ate.

The last words that were ever said
By Henry's disappearing head,
In accents of indignant scorn,
Were 'I am not a unicorn'.

And now you know why Henry sleeps,
And why his Mother mourns and weeps,
And why she also weeps and mourns;
So now be kind to unicorns.

XI

TO HIS GODSON, GERALD C. A. JACKSON

Aids to answering the first question in the Catechism.

When C. J. G. Arden goes out in the garden,
　　To play with the slugs and snails,
Their lives are imperilled by C. A. J. Gerald,
　　Who treads on their backs and their tails.
Their tails and their backs on, treads G. C. A. Jackson,
　　And each of them squirms and exclaims,
'Oh, G. A. J. Christopher, see how I twist over,
　　Under your numerous names.'

XII

FRAGMENT OF AN ENGLISH OPERA

(Designed as a model for young librettists)

Dramatis personae:
Father (bass)
Mother (contralto)
Daughter (soprano)

Scene: a Room. *Time*: Evening

Father:	Retire, my daughter; Prayers have been said; Take your warm water And go to bed.
Daughter:	But I had rather Sit up instead.
Father:	I am your father, So go to bed.
Daughter:	Are you my father?
Father:	I think so, rather: You go to bed.
Mother:	My daughter, vanish; You hear me speak: This is not Spanish, Nor is it Greek.

242

Daughter:	Oh, what a bother!
	Would I were dead!
Mother:	I am your mother,
	So go to bed.
Daughter:	Are you my mother?
Mother:	You have no other:
	You go to bed.

Father:	Take your bed-candle
	And take it quick.
	This is the handle.
Daughter:	Is *this* the handle?
Father:	No, that's the wick.
	This is the handle,
	At this end here.
	Take your bed-candle
	And disappear.
Daughter:	Oh dear, oh dear!
Father & Mother:	Take your warm water,
	As we have said;
	You are our daughter,
	So go to bed.
Daughter:	Am I your daughter?
Father & Mother:	If not, you oughter:
	You go to bed.

Daughter:	I am their daughter;
	If not, I oughter:

243

Prayers have been said.
This is my mother;
I have no other:
   Would I were dead!
That is my father;
He thinks so, rather:
   Oh dear, oh dear!
I take my candle;
This is the handle:
   I disappear.
Father & Mother: The coast is clear.

XIII

FRAGMENT OF A DIDACTIC POEM ON LATIN GRAMMAR

See on the cliff fair Adjectiva stand,
Roll the blue eye and wave the ivory hand;
Her amber locks refulgent emeralds deck
And orient sapphires wind her whiter neck.
She marks afar the much-loved youth pursue
O'er verdant meads the bounding kangaroo:
' 'Tis he! 'tis he! your wings, ye zephyrs, give!
Waft, waft me, breezes, to my Substantive!'
She speaks, and, headlong from the dizzy height,
Prone to the plain precipitates her flight.
Three nymphs attend her in the airy chase,
The nymphs of Number, Gender, and of Case;
The vine, the myrtle, and the rose they twine,
To bind thy victim, Concord, to the shrine.
The startled swain, in momentary dread,
As the fond fair descends upon his head,
Shouts: the high rocks his lusty outcry swell
And teach the obedient echoes how to yell.
Barks the pleased hound, spectator of the sport,
And hippopotami forget to snort.
On dove-borne car descends the Cyprian queen,
And hovering Cupids mitigate the scene.

The enamoured pair confess their mutual flame,
In gender, number, and in case the same;
Embowering roses screen their transports fond,
And simpering Syntax waves her jewelled wand.

So, up the steep side of the rugged hill,
Companions in adventure, Jack and Jill
With footing nice and anxious effort hale
To the moist pump the necessary pail.
The industrious pair their watery task divide,
And woo the bashful Naiad side by side.
The sturdier swain, for arduous labour planned,
The handle guiding in his practised hand,
With art hydraulic and propulsion stout
Evokes the crystal treasure from the spout,
The maid attentive to the useful flow,
Adjusts the apt receptacle below;
The gelid waves with bright reflections burn,
And mirrored beauty blushes in the urn.
Now down the slope, their task accomplished, they
The liquid plunder of the pump convey,
And seek the level sward; incautious pair!
Too soon, alas, too soon shall ye be there.
The hero first the strong compulsion feels,
And finds his head supplanted by his heels;
In circles whirled he thunders to the plain,
Vain all his efforts, all his language vain,
Vain his laced boots and vain his eyebrow dark,
And vain, ah! vain, his vaccination mark.

The inverted pail his flying form pursues,
With humid tribute and sequacious dews:
(So, through affrighted skies, o'er nations pale,
Behind the comet streams the comet's tail).
The prudent fair, of equilibrium vain,
Views, as he falls, the rotatory swain.
Exhilaration heaves her bosom young,
Tilts the fine nose, protrudes the vermeil tongue,
Bids from her throat the silvery laughters roll
And cachinnations strike the starry pole.
Gnomes! her light foot your envious fingers trip,
And freeze the titter on the ruby lip;
The massy earth with strong attraction draws,
And Venus yields to gravitation's laws;
From rock to rock the charms of Beauty bump,
And shrieks of anguish chill the conscious pump.

THE NOTE-BOOKS

THE NOTE-BOOKS

THE four note-books containing the original drafts of the bulk of A.E.H.'s poems, and also a few fair copies in the actual form in which they were published, cannot all be definitely divided in date; and though I have made a guess and distinguished them by the letters A, B, C and D, I cannot be sure that they came to be used in that order: except for A, which is certainly the first, since it contains three of the earliest poems (one dating as far back as 1890), and also more *Shropshire Lad* poems and fewer *Last Poems* than any of the three others.

These note-books cannot, in spite of their extreme interest for students, be preserved in their entirety. Under my brother's instructions all poems that are below a certain standard, and any unfinished verses, must be destroyed; and in making the accompanying selection (additional and final) of complete poems and verses I have gone as far as my conscience allows me, and rather farther than others have advised. In so doing I cannot hope to escape blame, on the one hand from those who will think I have selected too many, and on the other from those who would wish me not to have selected at all but to have given full measure, however unequal the material. But it is only the former blame that I shall mind; since it would so likely have been my brother's; and my duty is mainly to him.

But while I am not free to keep for myself, or to place in safe keeping for posterity, these intimate records of A.E.H.'s work as a whole, I may fortunately preserve from destruction the fair copies of such poems as have been published; and though I feel sure that my brother would not wish the workshop process by which he brought his verses to perfection to be exposed in detail, I think I may give an example or two of how, and with what delicacy of selection, some of his famous lines and phrases came to be written, so that even alternatives of fine quality suffered rejection – such, for instance, as the following variant of the first four lines of 'Tarry, delight, so seldom met', which, though written quite separately, obviously belongs to that poem both in thought and form:

> Joy, take my hand, talk to my heart,
>   Fold here awhile your wings and stay.
> Soon but not yet must we depart
>   To west and east away.

I cannot reproach myself for preserving that beautiful alternative, even though A.E.H. eventually preferred the other version.

I have already given my brother's account of how 'coloured counties' came to be written. There are in the note-books plenty of other instances to show that the right word came with difficulty, and how, out of many, the right one was always chosen. Take for example the description of the clock striking the quarters in the *Eight o'Clock* poem:

One, two, three four, to market place and people
    It tossed them down.

'Tossed' was only arrived at after the following had been tried and rejected: loosed, spilt, cast, told, dealt, and pitched.

In the second line of the last verse of 'Be still, my soul, be still' (No. XLVIII of *A Shropshire Lad*) 'All thoughts to rive the heart are here and all are vain': 'rive' was reached by way of no fewer than eight alternatives: vex, plague, tear, wrench, rend, wring, break, and pierce.

The lovely penultimate line of 'The lads in their hundreds to Ludlow come in for the fair', which runs:

They carry back bright to the coiner the mintage of man

had in the first draft only got to this: 'They carry unspoilt into safety the honour of man'. Surely in that change one sees in a flash inspiration at work.

It is worth noting that most of the finest of his poems came with most difficulty, or anyway were subjected to most correction; and so greatly were they changed for the better in the final form that, as first drafted, some would have come almost below standard. This applies especially to the following poems, which many would reckon among his best: 'On Wenlock Edge the wood's in trouble', 'Is my team ploughing', 'Be still, my soul, be still', 'Loveliest of trees, the cherry now', 'The lads in their hundreds to Ludlow', and 'Shot? so quick, so clean an ending?' And (to give a single example) here, for comparison, are the first and second drafts of the ninth stanza of *The Merry Guide*:

(*First version*)

> By windy shires of woodland
> With steeples dim-revealed,
> And cloudy shadows racing
> On all the endless weald.

(*Second version*)

> By blowing realms of woodland
> With sun-struck vanes afield
> And cloud-led shadows sailing
> About the windy weald.

Here the increased strength arising from the use of the two composite adjectives 'sun-struck' and 'cloud-led' is remarkable; but there is improvement in every line and in every change of word.

This power of self-criticism, with extraordinarily successful results, is noticeable through the manuscripts, which often run into three or four drafts with improvements all the way. One very striking improvement was the omission from *Eight o'Clock* of a third verse, good in itself but lessening the dramatic effect of the end of verse two.

It is interesting to note that the poem of which he made the most numerous fair copies (these always in ink, the first drafts being in pencil) was one of the very earliest – *The Sage to the Young Man*; it appears side by side with the first draft of *The Merry Guide*, but the last fair copy comes much later. Most readers will agree that of those two poems of the same date (1890) *The Merry Guide* is greatly the superior. *Bredon Hill*

(1891) is the earliest of the poems that have place-names attached to them; it is Worcestershire, not Shropshire. Another of the early poems, ''Tis time, I think, by Wenlock town', had 'Stourbridge town' in the first draft; greater beauty of sound may have decided the change into Shropshire, but A.E.H. admitted that his choice of locality was often haphazard and sometimes fictitious.

Hughley steeple was not the only place-name that he chose merely for sound. In Note-book A an early draft of the opening line of *A Shropshire Lad* gives 'On Wenlock Edge the beacon burns', which was changed later into 'From Clee to heaven'. Possibly he found that he needed 'On Wenlock Edge' for the opening of the later poem which has it.

I fear that these few notes of what the MSS. have to tell of A.E.H.'s methods of composition will be received with mixed feelings by those who resent the order for destruction of which I have to be the instrument. No one can be more sorry than I am that it has to be. One characteristic bit of destruction had already taken place before the note-books came into my possession; a page had been torn out. I surmise that on that page was written the last poem in *A Shropshire Lad* about which, in *The Name and Nature of Poetry*, A.E.H. set his readers a riddle, as to which of the verses were composed first and which last. He refused more than once to tell anyone the answer; I suspect that the answer was on the missing page, and that he purposely cancelled it, in order that his riddle might remain unsolved.

THE NOTE-BOOKS

ANALYSIS OF CONTENTS

Note-book A

After five pages of epigrammatical sentences, forty-eight pages are alternately occupied by classical notes to the right, nonsense verses to the left. After page 53 the rough drafts of the poems begin, and interspersed by a few fair copies occupy all the remainder, except the last ten pages, on which (starting from the other end) are more classical notes of reference.

In the following analysis the word 'fragment', unless qualified, stands for material which forms no part of the published poems.

Pages

54 A table of rhymes; and a single verse of 'O youth whose heart is right'.

55–7 Single lines and fragments.

58–9 'For these of old the trader' (fair copy), and the last line of 'Easter Hymn'.

60–2 'Stay if you list, O passer by the way', and fragments.

63 'Into my heart an air that kills' (fair copy, slightly corrected).

64–5 'When Israel out of Egypt came'.

66–7 Single lines and fragments.

68   'How clear, how lovely bright'.

69–76   Single lines and fragments.

77   'When Israel out of Egypt came' (two verses amended).

78–81   Fragments of 'God's Acre' with variants.

82–3   'There pass the careless people' (with two cancelled verses).

84–5   'Bring, in this timeless grave to throw' (rough draft).

86–7   Fragments.

88   'Yon fire that frets the eastern sky'.

89   'Like mine, the veins of these that slumber' (fair copy, slightly corrected).

90–105   Single lines and fragments.

106–9   'Once in the wind of morning' (dated Sept. 1890).

110–11   'O youth whose heart is right' (with three cancelled verses).

112   Single lines.

113   'I wake from dreams and turning' (with two cancelled verses).

114–15   'Once in the wind of morning' (corrected copy, dated Sept. 1890).

116–17   'Bring, in this timeless grave to throw' (fair copy, with further corrections).

118–23   Single lines and fragments.

124–5   ''Tis time, I think, by Stourbridge Town' (first draft). 'The fairies break their dances' (one verse), and fragments.

R

126–31 Fragments.

132–3 'In summertime on Bredon' (rough draft, dated July 1891).

134–5 'Far in a western brookland' (rough draft, and fair copy, dated 1891–2).

136–9 'O youth whose heart is right' (two fair copies, with corrections: two verses cancelled).

140–1 Single lines.

142–3 'In summertime on Bredon' (fair copy, with corrections).

144–5 'The farms of home lie lost in even', 'From far, from eve and morning', and 'He standing hushed, a pace or two apart'.

146–7 'Be still, my soul, be still' (rough draft, many corrections).

148 'If truth in hearts that perish' (rough draft).

149–50 Fragments, and the last verse of 'By shores, and woods and steeples'.

151 'The weeping Pleiads wester' (rough draft, and fair copy, dated Feb. 1893).

152–3 Unfinished poem of several verses (much corrected, three cancelled).

154 Fragments.

155 ''Tis time, I think, by Wenlock town' (fair copy, dated Feb. 1893).

155–7 'With rue my heart is laden' (dated Aug. 1893) and fragments.

158 'From far, from eve and morning' (fair copy, slightly corrected).

159   'Be still, my soul, be still' (second draft with corrections).

160   'I wake from dreams and turning' (fair copy).

161   'When he's returned I'll tell him'.

162–3   'Give me a land of boughs in leaf', the last line of 'The street sounds to the soldiers' tread', and fragments.

164   'You smile upon your friend to-day' (rough draft, all but the last verse cancelled).

165   'If truth in hearts that perish' (rough draft, two verses cancelled).

166–7   Fragments.

168–9   'Shake hands, we shall never be friends' (rough draft).

170   'The sun at noon to higher air' (rough draft).

171–3   Unfinished narrative poem, much corrected.

174–5   'Stars, I have seen them fall', and fragments.

176–7   'O youth whose heart is right' (corrected copy, one verse cancelled).

180   Fragments.

181   'White in the moon the long road lies' (rough draft).

182–3   Fragments, and single lines.

184   'Half-way for one commandment broken'.

185   'Because I liked you better' (rough draft, much corrected, and fragments).

186   'By shores and woods and steeples' (one verse cancelled).

187–9   An unfinished poem, fragments, and a few couplets from 'Terence, this is stupid stuff'.

190 Fragments.

191 'Farewell to barn and stack and tree' (dated Aug. 1894).

192 'The star-filled seas are smooth to-night', and two lines from 'Along the field as we came by'.

193 'The vane on Hughley steeple'.

194-7 Unfinished narrative poem (much corrected).

198-9 'If in that Syrian garden ages slain'.

200 Single lines.

201 'The laws of God, the laws of man'.

202-3 'From Clee to heaven the beacon burns' (rough draft, much corrected, several verses cancelled).

204 Nine lines from 'As through the wild green hills of Wyre'.

205 'Leave your home behind, lad' (two verses), and five lines from 'Her strong enchantments failing'.

206 'The lads in their hundreds to Ludlow' (two lines).

207 'Now hollow fires burn out to black', and 'Because I liked you better'.

208 'Oh see how thick the goldcup flowers' (two verses).

209 'In midnights of November' (three verses).

210-11 'The lad came to the door at night' (rough draft, dated December 1894).

212-13 'The lad came to the door at night' (fair copy).

214-15 'Home is the sailor, home from sea' (published in a periodical).

216 'He is here, Urania's son' (six lines) and 'When I was one-and-twenty' (single line, with date Jan. 1895). This is followed by a cut-out page of which

only the initial letters of nine lines remain, but
showing that it was a rough draft of the same
poem.

217 'High the vanes of Shrewsbury gleam' (three
verses, dated Jan. 1895).

218–19 'Wake: the silver dusk returning' (rough draft
much corrected, dated Jan. 1895).

220–1 Fragments, and two last lines of 'Westward on
the high-hilled plains'.

222–5 'Leave your home behind, lad' (rough draft, and
fair copy, dated Jan. 1895)

226 'Good creatures, do you love your lives'.

227 'On moonlit heath and lonesome bank' (rough
draft, dated Feb. 1895).

228–9 'When I meet the morning beam' (rough draft).

230 'When I watch the living meet'.

231 Unfinished narrative poem, and two lines from
'The winds out of the westland blow'.

232 'Look not in my eyes, for fear'.

233 'The winds out of the westland blow'.

234–5 Fragments and single lines.

236–7 'Far I hear the bugles blow' (rough draft, and
fair copy, dated March 1895).

238 'Others, I am not the first' (rough draft).

239 Fragments.

240–1 'The time you won your town the race' (rough
draft, five verses).

Note-book B

36 'Along the field as we came by' (dated June –).

37 'Shake hands, we shall never be friends'.

38–9 'It is no gift I tender' (dated June 1895)

40–1 'In valleys of springs of rivers'.

42–4 Fragments.

45 'When I came last to Ludlow' (dated June 1895).

46 'It nods and curtseys and recovers'.

47–8 ''Tis five years since, "An end, said I"' (fair copy).

49 'Here the hangman stops his cart' (last two lines).

50 Fragment.

51–2 'You smile upon your friend today'.

53–4 'Here the hangman stops his cart' (dated August, 1895).

55–6 Fragments.

57–8 'As through the wild green hills of Wyre' (rough draft, many corrections).

59 'The winds out of the westland blow'.

60–3 'Shot? so quick, so clean an ending' (rough draft)

64–5 Ditto (fair copy, slightly corrected).

66 'If it chance your eye offend you'.

67 'Wake: the silver dusk returning' (second verse only, with corrections).

68–9 'Is my team ploughing' (second draft, two verses much corrected).

70–1 'Oh, who is that young fellow' (rough draft).

72–3 'When I meet the morning beam'.

74–5 'When smoke stood up from Ludlow' (rough draft).

76 'Her strong enchantments failing' (fair copy).

77 'O fair enough are sky and plain'.

78–83 'Morning up the eastern stair', and variants (dated Sept. 1895).

84–7 'Terence, this is stupid stuff'.

88 'In the morning, in the morning'.

89 'When the lad for longing sighs'.

90 'Think no more, lad; laugh, be jolly'.

91 'Tarry, delight, so seldom met' (rough draft) with alternative to opening lines.

92 'Say, lad, have you things to do'.

93 'Oh, on my breast in days hereafter', and fragments.

94 'On the idle hill of summer' (fair copy).

95–6 'In midnights of November' (rough draft, four verses and fragments, dated Oct. 1895).

97–8 'On Wenlock Edge the wood's in trouble' (rough draft, many lines cancelled, dated Nov. 1895).

99–100 'The lads in their hundreds to Ludlow' (two rough drafts).

101–8 Fragments and single lines.

109–10 'In my own shire, if I was sad' (rough draft, many lines cancelled, dated Nov. 1895).

111–12 Fragments of 'The chestnut casts his flambeaux'.

113 Unpublished poem.

114–15 'Oh, sick I am to see you'.

116–17 'Yonder see the morning blink' (dated Dec. 1895).

118–22 Single lines and fragments.

123 'The chestnut casts his flambeaux' (rough draft of first verse). Single lines and fragments.

124 'Ask me no more, for fear I should reply', and single lines.

125-6 Single lines and fragments.

127-8 'The night my father got me' (rough draft).

129 'When first my way to fair I took' (last verse and another cancelled).

130-1 Fragments and single lines.

132 'Smooth between sea and land' (rough draft of three verses, and single lines).

133-5 Fragments and single lines.

136 Fragments of 'I 'listed at home for a lancer'.

137-8 'Beyond the moor and mountain crest' (rough draft of six verses, much corrected and cancelled).

139-43 Fragments and single lines.

144 'The skies, they are not always raining' (second verse).

145-6 The dedicatory poem for his *Manilius*, in Latin elegiacs, addressed to M. J. Jackson (rough draft).

147-9 Fragments and single lines.

150-1 An unpublished poem (much corrected, several verses cancelled).

152-3 'The orchards half the way' (rough draft).

154-5 'They say my verse is sad: no wonder', and fragments.

156-7 Fragments and single lines.

158-9 'Here dead lie we because we did not choose' (two versions) and fragments.

160 'When first my way to fair I took'.

161 'The fairies break their dances'.

162–8 'When the bells justle in the tower', fragments and single lines.

169 'Now dreary dawns the eastern light' (second verse).

170–1 'The orchards half the way' (fair copy, slightly corrected).

172–3 'When lads were home from labour' (rough draft of three verses), and fragments.

174 'To stand up straight and tread the turning mill' and 'Now to her (lap) the incestuous earth'.

175–6 'The rain, it streams on stone and hillock' (rough draft) and fragments.

177–8 'Oh stay at home, my lad, and plough' (rough draft, and fair copy).

179 'West and away the wheels of darkness roll' (rough draft of second verse), and fragments.

180 Fragments.

181–4 'Beyond the moor and mountain crest' (rough draft, and second draft much corrected).

185–6 Unpublished poem (rough draft and fair copy).

187 Single lines.

188–9 'I walked alone and thinking' (rough draft of four verses).

190–2 'Oh hard is the bed they have made him' (rough draft and fair copy).

193–4 Single lines and fragments.

195 'The Queen she sent to look for me.'

196–7 'He would not stay for me', fragments and single lines.

198–9 Fragments

200–1   Latin dedicatory poem (second draft).

202–3   ''Tis mute, the word they went to hear'.

204–5   'What sound awakened me, I wonder' (rough draft of three verses), and fragments.

206   Fragment.

207–8   'Star and coronal and bell' (rough draft).

209–10   'When lads were home from labour' (rough draft of three verses).

211–14   Fragments and single lines.

215   'Farewell to a name and a number'.

216–17   Fragments and single lines.

218   'I lay me down and slumber'.

219–20   'When lads were home from labour' (fair copy with corrections).

221   'The Wain upon the northern steep'.

222   'The stars have not dealt me the worst they could do' (rough draft, much corrected).

223–4   'Lydians, lords of Hermus river' (rough draft, much corrected).

225   'The rainy Pleiads wester'.

226   'Some can gaze and not be sick', and fragments.

227   'The sigh that heaves the grasses', and fragments.

228   'Sons of landsmen, sons of seamen' (rough draft of four verses).

229–31   'The olive in its orchard' (rough draft and fair copy of verses published in a periodical, dated 1902).

The rest of the note-book is taken up by 16 pages of tabulated rhymes, and vowel sounds, under various headings.

Note-book C

55   Unpublished poem.

56–7   'Ho, everyone that thirsteth' (one verse cancelled).

58   Fragments and single lines.

59   'Crossing alone the nighted ferry'.

60–9   Fragments and single lines.

70–1   'Wake not for the world-heard thunder', fragments.

72–80   Fragments and single lines.

81   'Onward led the road again' (five lines).

82–8   Fragments and single lines.

89   'We'll to the woods no more' (rough draft of first
four lines).

90–1   'When summer's end is nighing' (rough draft).

92–3   'These in the day when heaven was falling'
(rough draft, and second draft corrected).

94–5   'Oh, were he and I together'.

96–9   'He stood and heard the steeple' (rough draft,
three verses, second draft with verse cancelled, fair
copy).

100–5   Single lines.

106   Unpublished poem.

107   'We'll to the woods no more' (eight lines).

108–12   Fragments and single lines.

Note-book D

39–40 'Star and coronal and bell' (fair copy).

41–2 'What sound awakened me, I wonder' (fair copy, one verse much corrected and cancelled).

43 'The laws of God, the laws of man' (fair copy).

44–6 'The chestnut casts his flambeaux' (second draft with corrections).

47–8 'The stars have not dealt me the worst they could do'.

49–50 'The chestnut casts his flambeaux' (fair copy).

51–2 'Tarry, delight, so seldom met' (fragment and fair copy).

53–5 'In valleys green and still' (rough draft and fair copy).

56 'The rainy Pleiads wester' (fair copy).

57–60 'He is here, Urania's son' (two rough drafts and fair copy).

62 Unpublished poem.

63–4 'If in that Syrian garden, ages slain' (fragment, and fair copy).

65 'Her strong enchantments failing' (fair copy).

66 'Stone, steel, dominions pass' (second draft, and fair copy).

67–76 'Onward led the road again' (rough draft, second draft and fair copy, last page dated 10 April, 1922).

77 'I promise nothing: friends will part'.

78–9 'Far-known to sea and shore' (rough draft).

80–1 'The mill-stream, now that noises cease'.

82–3 'The rain, it streams on stone and hillock' (fragments, and fair copy).

84–5 'In midnights of November' (fair copy).

90 'The night is freezing fast'.

91–2 Unpublished poem (rough draft).

93 Fragments.

94–5 'Young is the blood that yonder' (rough draft).

96 'Far-known to sea and shore' (fair copy).

97–8 'Oh is it the jar of nations' (rough draft and fair copy).

99 'The sloe was lost in flower'.

100–1 'Tell me not, it needs not saying' (fair copy).

102–4 Fragments.

105–6 'Bells in tower at evening tell', and fragments.

107–8 'The rain, it streams on stone and hillock' (fair copy, amended version), and fragments.

109–11 Fragments and single lines.

112 'O thou that from thy mansion' (fair copy dated Jan. 1925).

113–15 Unpublished poem and fragments.

116 Dream poem (with note).

117 'I did not lose my heart on summer's even' (fair copy).

118 Unpublished poem.

119 'The world goes none the lamer' (fair copy).

120 'I to my perils' (fair copy).

121–2 'Young is the blood that yonder' (fair copy).

123 'Crossing alone the nighted ferry' (fair copy with corrections).

124–5 Fragments.

Starting from the other end are six pages of nonsense rhymes.

COMPLETE LIST OF DATED POEMS

COMPLETE LIST OF DATED POEMS

Twenty-five of the following dates were entered in the
note-books; all the rest, except the date of 'For my Funeral',
were supplied by A.E.H. to Sir Sydney Cockerell.

A Shropshire Lad

Once in the wind of morning	Sept. 1890
In summertime on Bredon (first draft)	July 1891
Far in a western brookland	1891–2
'Tis time, I think, by Wenlock Town	Feb. 1893
With rue my heart is laden	Aug. 1893
Farewell to barn and stack and tree	Aug. 1894
The lad came to the door at night (first draft)	Dec. 1894
When I was one-and-twenty (first draft)	Jan. 1895
Wake: the silver dusk returning (first draft)	Jan. 1895
Leave your home behind, lad	Jan. 1895
High the vanes of Shrewsbury gleam	Jan. 1895
On moonlit heath and lonesome bank (first draft)	Feb. 1895
Far I hear the bugle blow	Mar. 1895
'Tis spring; come out to ramble	Apr. 1895
Oh, when I was in love with you	May 1895
Along the field as we came by	June (1895?)
When I came last to Ludlow	July 1895
Here the hangman stops his cart	Aug. 1895

A Shropshire Lad — continued
> In my own shire, if I was sad (first draft) Nov. 1895
> On Wenlock Edge the wood's in trouble
> > > (first draft) Nov. 1895

Last Poems.
> Her strong enchantments failing   1895
> Yonder see the morning blink   Dec. 1895
> In the morning, in the morning   1895
> In midnights of November Begun 1895, Finished 1905
> The chestnut casts his flambeaux Feb. 1896:
> > > last verse, April 1922
> Oh hard is the bed they have made him Before 1899
> The laws of God, the laws of man   *c.* 1900
> As I gird on for fighting   *c.* 1900
> When the eye of day is shut   Aug. 1900
> The fairies break their dances   *c.* 1900–1905
> Could man be drunk for ever   *c.* 1900–1905
> Star and coronal and bell   1900–1922
> He is here, Urania's son   Begun 1900,
> > > Finished Apr. 1922
> The sigh that heaves the grasses   Soon after 1900
> I 'listed at home for a lancer   Time of Boer War
> The Queen she sent to look for me Time of Boer War
> The rain, it streams on stone and hillock *c.* 1902–1922
> Oh stay at home, my lad, and plough. After Boer War
> 'Tis mute, the word they went to hear   *c.* 1903[1]
> The Wain upon the northern steep   Before 1904

> [1] A.E.H. gave date *c.* 1904; but this poem appeared in *The Venture* in 1903.

Beyond the moor and mountain crest   *c.* 1905
Soldier from the wars returning   Chiefly 1905
The orchards half the way   *c.* 1905
Onward led the road again   1905–Apr. 1922
What sound awakened me, I wonder   Begun 1905,
     Finished Apr. 1922
When first my way to fair I took   Before 1910
The night my father got me   Before 1910
I walked alone and thinking   1910–1922
When I would muse in boyhood   After 1910
When summer's end is nighing   1920–1922
He stood, and heard the steeple   1921
West and away   First stanza, 1922, others earlier
Wake not for the world-heard thunder 30 Mar., 1922
We'll to the woods no more   Apr. 1922
In valleys green and still (except for last
   verse, written long previously)   Apr. 1922
The night is freezing fast   Apr. 1922
The sloe was lost in flower   Finished Apr. 1922
The half-moon westers low, my love   Apr. 1922
Tell me not here, it needs not saying   Apr. 1922

More Poems

The weeping Pleiads wester   Feb. 1893
O thou that from thy mansion   Jan. 1925

Now first published

It is no gift I tender   June 1895
Morning up the eastern stair   Sept. 1895

THE NATAL HOROSCOPE

OF

A. E. HOUSMAN

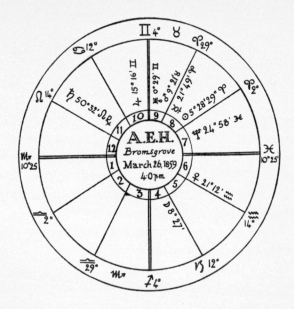

PLANET	☉	☽	☿	♀	♂	♃	♄	♅	♇	Declin⁰	Ruler ☿	Rising *None*
☉	–	□	–	∠	–	–	△	–	P	2°11'N	F 3	
☽	□	–	–	–	△	–	–	–	–	27°6'S	E 2	
☿	–	–	–	✳	–	–	–	–	–	9°41'N	A 3	Triplicities
♀	∠	–	✳	–	P	△	–	–	–	14°5'S	W 1	
♂	–	△	–	P	–	–	□	–	∠	14°52'N	Card 3	
♃	–	–	–	△	–	–	–	–	–	22°22'N	Fixed 3	Quadruplicities
♄	△	–	–	–	□	–	–	P	–	19°43'N	Mutable 3	
♅	–	–	–	–	–	–	P	–	–	20°8'N	Angular 3	
♇	P	–	–	–	∠	–	–	–	–	3°5'S	Succeedent 3	Mundane
A sc.	–	△	–	–	△	□	–	–	–		Cadent 3	
M.C.	✳	–	∠	–	–	–	✳	♂	–			

Essential Dignities
House *None*
Detriment ♂♃♄☽
Exaltation ☉
Fall *None*

HOROSCOPE OF A. E. HOUSMAN

Character. The character is fundamentally an exceptionally well balanced one as between energy and initiative, stability and patience, and sensitiveness and versatility. (Planets equally divided among cardinal, fixed, and mutable signs.) A similar balance is shown by the arrangement of the planets in respect of the triplicities. There is a preponderance of energy, passion, and emotion, combined with an equal degree of refinement, love of the beautiful, and artistic taste and inspiration. (Three planets in fiery and three in airy signs.) But there is a solid basis of practical good sense and ability to deal with concrete details. (Two planets in earthy signs.) The artistic faculties are highly developed, and there is great love of beauty both in nature and in literature. (Venus ruler of third house and sextile to Mercury ruler.)

In the main you are careful and prudent and capable of exercising much forethought before acting. (Virgo rising. Sun trine to Saturn.) But at times you will let yourself go and show more impulse and energy than prudence or foresight. This will be due to a quickness of wit which is liable to express itself in sarcasm and may lead to trouble. (Mercury ruler in Aries.) In money matters you are on the whole prudent and economical, and the acquisitive side of your character is well developed. (Moon in Capricorn.) But you can be very

generous to friends (Sun in Aries), and in this connection
you might even be in danger of being extravagant.
(Moon trine to Mars.)

Natives born under Virgo generally tend to be too diffi-
dent and lacking in 'push', not hopeful enough and
rather inclined to give way in face of difficulties. In your
case these features, though they will certainly be present,
are largely neutralized by a number of other factors which
make for energy, confidence, and ambition. You are at
heart an extremely ambitious and aspiring person, with
an intense desire for fame and recognition. (Mercury
ruler in Aries. Sun in Aries. Moon in Capricorn.) You
like to be appreciated, and work best under the stimulus
of admiration. (Sun in Aries.) You do not over-estimate
your own abilities (Virgo rising. Moon in Capricorn), but
you are highly independent and fearless and are prepared
to take the responsibility for your own opinions and
actions. (Sun in Aries. Moon trine to Mars.)

In manner you will be quiet, retiring, modest, and
reserved. You are, in fact, kind and sympathetic, but you
do not wear your heart on your sleeve. You seldom show
your real nature openly, and are at times difficult to
understand. (Virgo rising.) You are, however, extremely magnanimous and loyal to your friends (Sun in
Aries), and are capable of dealing successfully with others
if you choose to attempt it. (Moon trine to Mars.)

At times you are apt to worry needlessly, to vacillate,
and to lose hope. (Virgo rising.) But you can also be
merry and cheerful, light-hearted and free, in company;

and you have the kind of character which will make you a notable figure in any company. (Mercury ruler sextile to Venus. Moon in Capricorn. Moon trine to Mars.)

You have a notable power of doing steady, patient, exact work; you are highly conscientious – a characteristic which will increase as you grow older; your character will always command respect for this reason, and you could hold very responsible positions if you cared to take them. (Sun trine to Saturn.) The character is a very capable one, and you could have done pretty well at anything within reason that you had set your hand to. (Moon in Capricorn.)

Intellect. The mental abilities are excellent. You are studious, and can learn a subject quickly. You could develop a fair amount of practical ability, if you chose, and you are able to attend to minute details with skill and method. (Virgo rising.) You can appreciate most intellectual pursuits, and you have a respect for intellectual achievements. (Mercury in Aries.) You have a logical mind, are apt and ingenious in argument, plausible and fluent in speech and writing, and could probably attain distinction as a writer or speaker. (Virgo rising. Mercury ruler in Aries.) You are very positive in your opinions, and cannot be convinced against your will. (Mercury in eighth house.) You are very independent in your thoughts and feelings, especially about religion or philosophy; you hold what are commonly regarded as very 'advanced' and 'unorthodox' opinions on these subjects; and you combat against any system of opinions of which you disapprove. (Mars and Uranus in ninth house.) Yet you have a considerable interest in mysticism and oc-cultism, and an intense curiosity and concern with death and after life. (Mercury ruler in eighth house.) You like exploring the unknown, and dwelling on subjects which are thought 'far-fetched' and 'superstitious', and are interested in astrology and kindred subjects. (Uranus in eighth house.) As you grow older you are likely to be-come more receptive to influences of this kind and more interested in mysticism. (Moon in fourth house.)

You have a good memory, plenty of wit, and great ingenuity and originality of mind. (Mercury ruler in Aries. Uranus in ninth house.) You combine great critical powers (Uranus in ninth house) and splendid intuitive judgment (Sun in Aries); but there is a danger of not keeping your criticisms at a purely impersonal level (Uranus in ninth house), especially as you are some-what self-assertive in intellectual things. (Mercury ruler in Aries.)

Along with these great positive gifts there are certain defects. You are somewhat lacking in mental concentra-tion and perseverance, and inclined to change too quickly and often from one subject to another. (Mercury ruler in Aries.) At times you tend to be over-anxious (Mercury in eighth house), and you will seldom enjoy much mental peace or calm. (Mars in ninth house.)

Friendship, Love, and Marriage. You are likely to make friends among literary people, and those associated with books and learning. (Mercury ruler in Aries.) You

are very loyal to all your friends (Sun in Aries), and faithful in all your attachments (Venus in Aquarius), and will
have some very faithful and reliable friends especially
among elderly people (Saturn in eleventh house). Yet
there are strong indications that you will have trouble
and many bitter disappointments in connection with
friendship and love. You will not have many *real*
friends. Many apparent ones will desert you when you
most need them. You will always need to be very
guarded in your dealings with persons who move your
affections, as you are particularly liable to be thwarted
and disappointed in this connection. (Sun semi-square
to Venus. Saturn in eleventh house.)

There is likely to be disappointment in love, and
marriage will be long delayed if ever it takes place.
There is a strong inclination for a celibate life, for you
would pitch your demands in love very high, and you
have the kind of intuition which would tell you when
these demands cannot be fulfilled and would prevent
you from making a false step. You are capable of very
faithful attachment and of waiting a long time; but some
kind of secret and irregular union is more likely than an
ordinary marriage. (Venus in Aquarius.) If the marriage
ever took place it would be of an unusual kind; it might
be with one who was in some way afflicted or crippled
physically, mentally, or morally. (Neptune in seventh
house.)

Health and End of Life. There was danger to health,
and even to life, in early infancy; but this was successfully

passed, and the energy and bodily strength increase as you grow older. (Ruler in eighth house.) The constitution is a good one, with considerable power of resistance to disease. (Moon trine to Mars.) The general health improves as life advances, and, if you are reasonably abstemious, you are likely to live to a very considerable age. (Sun trine to Saturn.) But health and vitality will suffer at times, and, in particular, you will always need to be careful of your eyesight. (Sun square to Moon.) Your chief danger is to wear yourself out by anxiety, mental activity or excitement, and worry. This will tend to result in neuralgia or severe headaches. (Mercury in Aries. Mercury in eighth house.) You are somewhat liable to illnesses which arise from excess or indiscretion in diet or habits of living. If health is affected from such causes, the kidneys, throat, and generative organs are likely to be affected. Temperance is essential if you are to keep in good health, and any illness will probably be traceable to some departure from it. (Venus in sixth house.)

Career. You are, on the whole, the kind of man who would do better as a servant than as a master in the practical affairs of life. (Virgo rising.) But you have the ability to take a leading part in mental activities, and are likely to make your mark by your intellectual powers either as a speaker or a writer. (Mercury ruler in Aries.) You will have the opportunity to bring out what is born in you, and are likely to raise yourself above the position in which you were born. (Seven planets above the horizon.) You will follow an honourable profession, by which you are likely to gain both financially and socially. Your occupation will be to your taste and will bring you success. (Jupiter in tenth house.) Nevertheless your life will not be a specially easy one. You will meet with many obstacles, and are likely often to be disappointed in your hopes and wishes, particularly where your feelings are involved. (Sun square to Moon and semi-square to Venus.) Though you will eventually become very well known in the circle in which you move (Moon in Capricorn), it is useless for you ever to expect wide popularity, and it would not be good for you if you had it. (Sun square to Moon.) At certain times in your life there will be monetary troubles; your environment has not always been easy, and there has been lack of content-ment and ease of mind. (Sun semi-square to Venus.) You need to exercise great tact and diplomacy in all your dealings with official superiors and persons in authority, and failure in this respect is likely to be at the root of the above mentioned troubles. (Sun square to Moon.) There have been and will be a great many changes in your life. Ties have been made and broken when you least desired it. It seems likely that changes and domestic worries and a good deal of general unsettlement will occur at the close of your life; but *all* your undertakings have a tendency to end in uncertainty. (Moon in fourth house.) You are likely to benefit from persons older than yourself, and to be helped in the course of your life by those holding important positions. (Sun trine to

Saturn.) You will have a good deal to do with wills and the property or affairs of the dead. In fact you will be brought in touch with death in a number of ways, and it is likely that you will be at some time influenced profoundly by the death of a friend or relative. (Ruler in eighth house.)

Financial Prospects. There is nothing very exciting under this head. Though there will be financial difficulties at times (Sun semi-square to Venus), there is nothing serious to be feared on financial grounds and you are likely to accumulate a reasonable competence by middle life, which will be your most fortunate period. (Jupiter in an angular house.) Acquisitiveness is well developed, and you have a certain amount of capacity for speculation. (Cardinal sign on cusp of second house.) You are pretty certain to benefit by legacy. (Ruler in eighth house, Sun in eighth house, Moon in fourth house.) The legacy might come either from a relative or from a social superior. (Sun in eighth.) You would gain financially through partnership with others or through marriage. (Ruler in eighth. Sun in eighth.) At some time you will have to act as administrator, executor, or trustee – very probably as a literary executor. (Mercury ruler in eighth house.)